PRACTICE BOOK

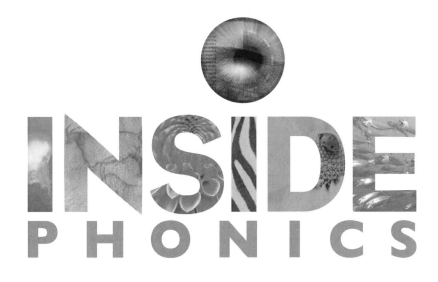

PRACTICE BOOK

INSIDE
PHONICS

NATIONAL
GEOGRAPHIC

Hampton-Brown

Acknowledgments

Grateful acknowledgment is given to the authors, artists, photographers, museums, publishers, and agents for permission to reprint copyrighted material. Every effort has been made to secure the appropriate permission. If any omissions have been made or if corrections are required, please contact the Publisher.

COVER DESIGN: (tc) argus/Shutterstock. (l - r) Stuart Westmoreland/Corbis. Christophe Boisvieux/Corbis. Clive Nichols/Corbis. Charlie Munsey/Corbis. Andrejs Pidjass/Shutterstock. Frans Lanting/Corbis.

PUBLISHED BY NATIONAL GEOGRAPHIC SCHOOL PUBLISHING & HAMPTON-BROWN
Sheron Long, Chief Executive Officer
Samuel Gesumaria, President

THE NATIONAL GEOGRAPHIC SOCIETY
John M. Fahey, Jr., President & Chief Executive Officer
Gilbert M. Grosvenor, Chairman of the Board

Manufacturing and Quality Management, The National Geographic Society
Christopher A. Liedel, Chief Financial Officer
George Bounelis, Vice President

National Geographic School Publishing
Hampton-Brown
P.O. Box 223220
Carmel, California 93922
www.NGSP.com

Printed in the United States of America
ISBN: 978-0-7362-6000-8

22 23 24 25   18 17 16 15 14 13 12

Contents

Foundations of Reading

Reading Practice

Contents

Reading Practice, continued

Contents

Decodable Passages

Tear-Out/Fold-Up Books

Foundations of Reading

▶ **Letters and Sounds**

A. Study the new letters and sounds.

Ss **Mm** **Ff** **Hh** **Tt** **Aa**

B. Say the name of each picture below. What letter spells the <u>first</u> sound you hear? Circle the letter.

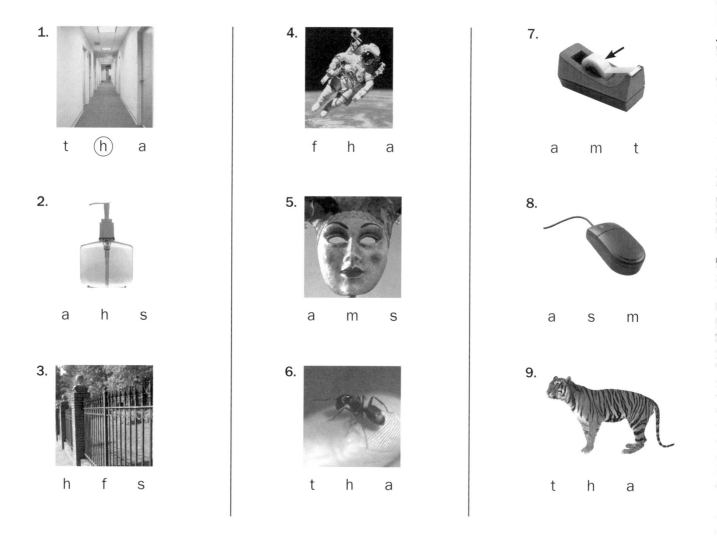

1. t (h) a

2. a h s

3. h f s

4. f h a

5. a m s

6. t h a

7. a m t

8. a s m

9. t h a

Foundations of Reading

▶ Letters and Sounds

Say the name of each picture below. What letter spells the <u>first</u> sound you hear? Write the letter.

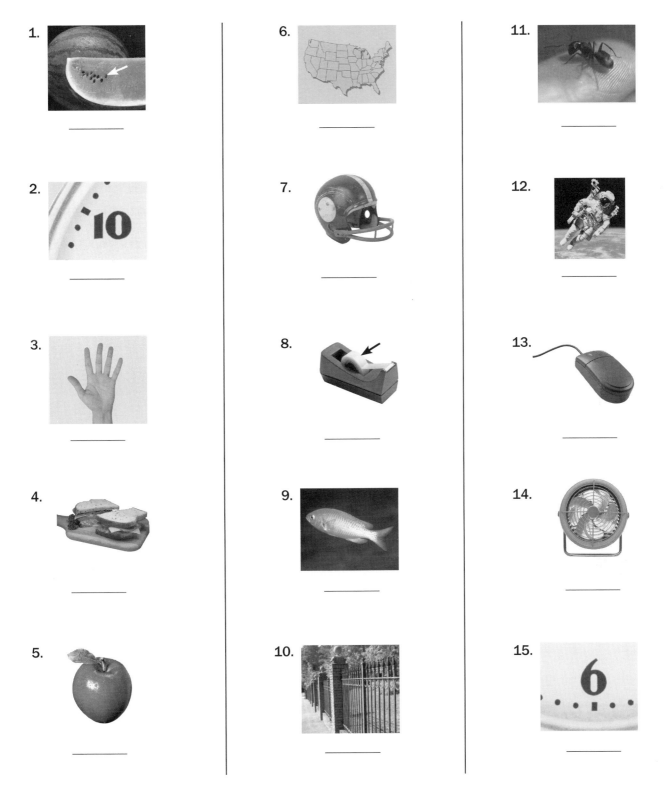

1. _____

2. _____

3. _____

4. _____

5. _____

6. _____

7. _____

8. _____

9. _____

10. _____

11. _____

12. _____

13. _____

14. _____

15. _____

Foundations of Reading

▶ **High Frequency Words**

Read each word. Then write it.

1. am	_____	4. school	_____
2. I	_____	5. the	_____
3. is	_____	6. this	_____

How to Play

1. Make a spinner.

2. Write the name of each player on a blank.

3. Spin. Read the sentence.

The first player to read all six sentences wins.

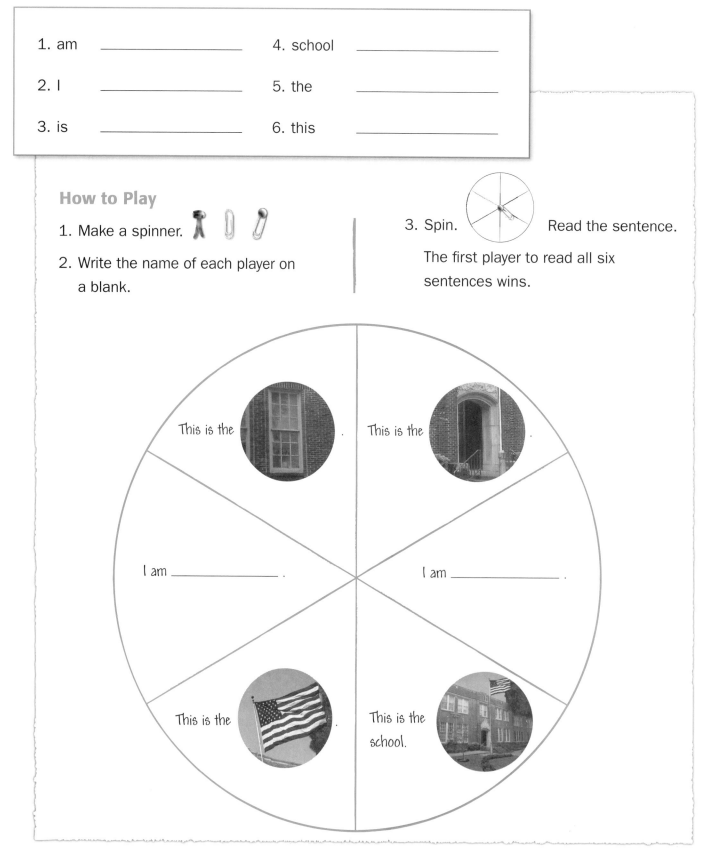

This is the _____.

This is the _____.

I am _____.

I am _____.

This is the _____.

This is the school.

Foundations of Reading

Name _____

▶ **High Frequency Words**

Read each word. Then write it.

1. a _____ 4. my _____

2. an _____ 5. no _____

3. here _____ 6. you _____

1. Find the words. Circle them.
   Look across. ➡

q	ⓐ	o	p	t	m
v	l	e	s	a	n
s	b	m	l	n	l
h	e	r	e	o	r
z	p	l	g	m	y
n	o	r	z	q	w
w	f	y	o	u	z
x	g	q	t	d	s

5. Find the words. Circle them.
   Look down. ⬇

a	q	h	j	z	t
n	v	e	u	n	s
k	s	r	r	o	g
l	b	e	h	o	y
r	a	i	z	e	o
x	f	s	m	r	u
w	g	o	y	e	q
p	u	z	e	l	v

Write the missing words.

2. Here is ___my___ 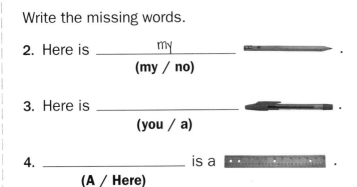 .
   (my / no)

3. Here is _____ .
   (you / a)

4. _____ is a .
   (A / Here)

Write the missing words.

6. This is ___an___ 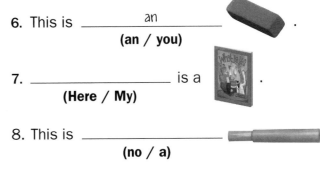 .
   (an / you)

7. _____ is a .
   (Here / My)

8. This is _____ .
   (no / a)

Foundations of Reading

Name _____

▶ **High Frequency Words**

A. Read each word. Then write it.

1. at	_____	4. of	_____
2. it	_____	5. on	_____
3. look	_____	6. yes	_____

B. Write the missing letters.

7. Which words have a **t**?

   a   t   ____ ____

8. Which words have 2 letters?

   ____ ____   ____ ____

   ____ ____   ____ ____

9. Which word has 3 letters?

   ____ ____ ____

10. Which word has 4 letters?

   ____ ____ ____ ____

11. Which words start with **o**?

   ____ ____   ____ ____

12. Which word has an **f**?

   ____ ____

C. Write the missing words.

13. Carlos, _____ at this!
    (of / look)

14. Is this the school?

    Yes, _____ is.
    (it / at)

15. I am _____ school.
    (at / of)

16. This is a _____
    (of / look)

    the school.

17. The [picture] is _____
    (it / on)

    the [chair] .

Name _____

► **Read on Your Own**

Read these sentences.

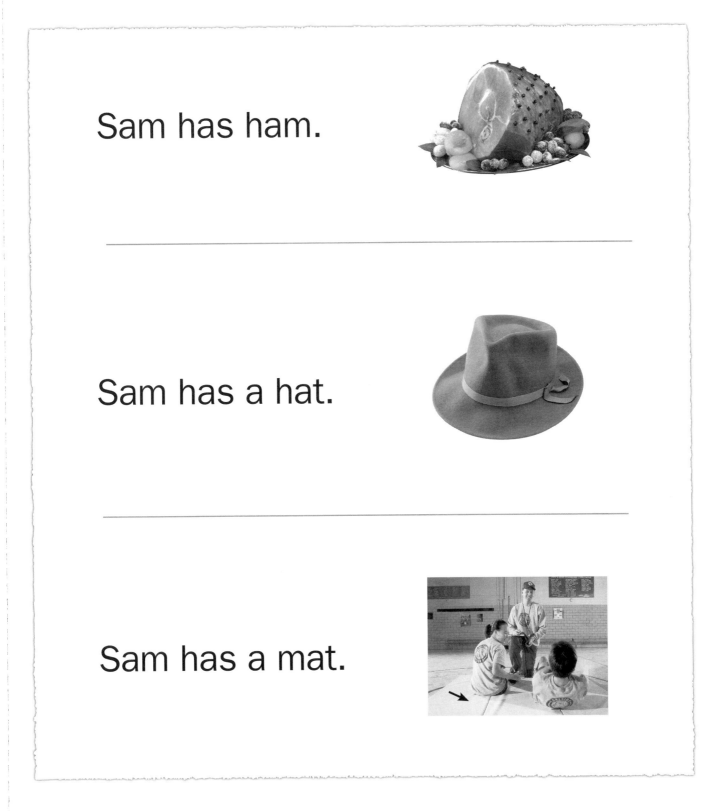

Sam has ham.

Sam has a hat.

Sam has a mat.

Foundations of Reading

Name _____

▶ Words with Short *a*

A. Read each word. Draw a line to match the word and the picture.

1.

hat

ham

2.

fat

mat

B. Write the missing words.

3.

This is a ___hat___ .
(ham / hat)

4.

Maylin is _____ school.
(at / sat)

5.

Here is the _____ .
(fat / mat)

6.

I _____ Ron.
(Sam / am)

7.

This is a _____ .
(ham / hat)

8.

You _____ at the .
(at / sat)

Foundations of Reading

Name _____

▶ Words with Short *a*

A. Write the missing *a*. Then read the words in each list. How are the words different?

1.

<u>a</u> m

S ___ m

h ___ m

2.

___ t

h ___ t

s ___ t

3.

___ t

f ___ t

m ___ t

B. What word completes each sentence and tells about the picture? Spell the word.

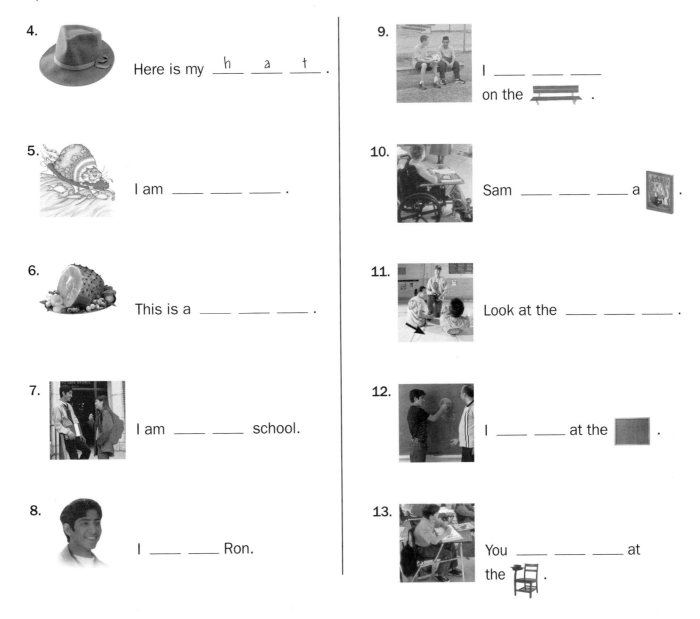

4.

Here is my <u>h</u> <u>a</u> <u>t</u> .

5.

I am ___ ___ ___ .

6.

This is a ___ ___ ___ .

7.

I am ___ ___ school.

8.

I ___ ___ Ron.

9.

I ___ ___ ___ on the ___ .

10.

Sam ___ ___ ___ a ___ .

11.

Look at the ___ ___ ___ .

12.

I ___ ___ at the ___ .

13.

You ___ ___ ___ at the ___ .

► Letters and Sounds

A. Study the new letters and sounds.

| Nn | Ll | Pp | Gg | Ii |

B. Say the name of each picture below. What letter spells the <u>first</u> sound you hear? Circle the letter.

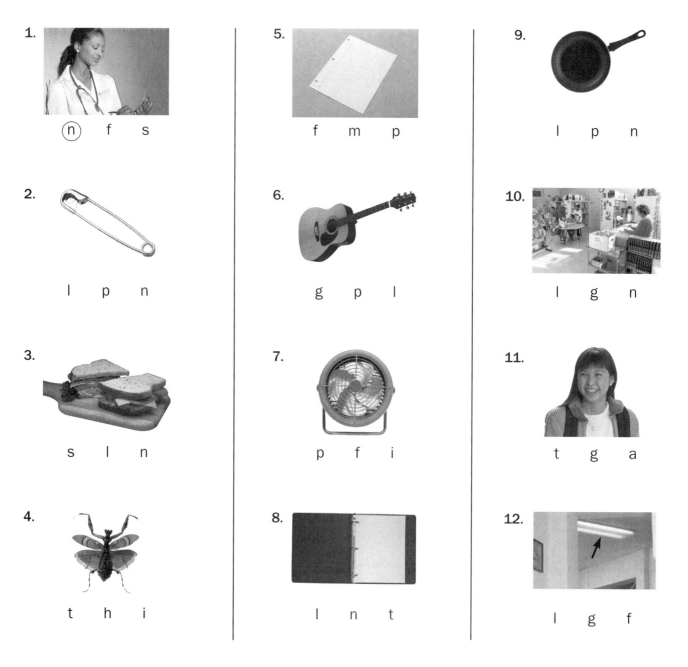

1. (n) f s

2. l p n

3. s l n

4. t h i

5. f m p

6. g p l

7. p f i

8. l n t

9. l p n

10. l g n

11. t g a

12. l g f

Foundations of Reading

Name _____

▶ **Letters and Sounds**

Say the name of each picture below. Write the missing letters.

1.

h   a   m

2.

___ ___ ___

3.

___ i ___

4.

s i ___

5.

___ i ___

6.

m ___ ___

7.

___ ___ ___

8.

___ ___ m p

9.

___ ___ ___

10.

m ___ ___

11.

___ i ___

12.

___ ___ ___

Foundations of Reading

Name _____

▶ **High Frequency Words**

A. Read each word. Then write it.

1. are _____   4. show _____

2. good _____   5. where _____

3. see _____   6. he _____

B. Write the missing letters.

7. Which words have 4 letters?

g o o d

___ ___ ___ ___

8. Which word has an **a**?

___ ___ ___

9. Which word has 5 letters?

___ ___ ___ ___ ___

10. Which words have 3 letters?

___ ___ ___

___ ___ ___

11. Which word has a **g**?

___ ___ ___ ___

12. Which words have a **w**?

___ ___ ___ ___ ___

___ ___ ___ ___

13. Which word has 2 letters?

___ ___

C. Write the missing word.

14. I _____ two pens.
(see / are)

15. Where _____ the people?
(are / he)

16. This is a _____ sandwich.
(good / see)

17. _____ me the motorcycle.
(Show / Where)

18. _____ is the boy?
(Show / Where)

19. We do not know who _____
is. **(see / he)**

© NGSP & HB

Foundations of Reading

Name _____

▶ High Frequency Words

A. Read each word. Then write it.

1. answer _____   4. time _____

2. she _____   5. who _____

3. some _____   6. your _____

B. Write the missing letters.

7. Which word has 6 letters?

   a   n   s   w   e   r
   ─── ─── ─── ─── ─── ───

8. Which words have an **m**?

   ─── ─── ─── ───

   ─── ─── ───

9. Which words have 3 letters?

   ─── ─── ───

   ─── ─── ───

10. Which words have 4 letters?

    ─── ─── ─── ───

    ─── ─── ─── ───

    ─── ─── ─── ───

11. Which words have a **w**?

    ─── ─── ─── ─── ─── ───

    ─── ─── ───

12. Which word has a **y**?

    ─── ─── ─── ───

C. Write the missing word.

13. I write the _____ .
    (answer / some)

14. _____ is my friend.
    (She / Your)

15. What _____ is class?
    (time / your)

16. _____ puppy is very cute.
    (Your / Who)

17. I have _____ homework.
    (some / who)

18. _____ do you see?
    (Who / She)

Name _____

▶ **High Frequency Words**

A. Read each word. Then write it.

1. point _____   4. with _____

2. read _____   5. work _____

3. to _____   6. write _____

B. Write the missing letters.

7. Which words have 4 letters?

___ ___ ___ ___

___ ___ ___ ___

___ ___ ___ ___

8. Which words have a **w**?

___ ___ ___ ___

___ ___ ___ ___

___ ___ ___ ___ ___

9. Which words have 5 letters?

___ ___ ___ ___ ___

___ ___ ___ ___ ___

10. Which word has a **k**?

___ ___ ___ ___

11. Which words have an **r**?

___ ___ ___ ___

___ ___ ___ ___

___ ___ ___ ___ ___

C. Write the missing word.

12. I _____ a book.
    (read / point)

13. I _____ to the answer.
    (work / point)

14. Carlos will _____ on
    (write / with)
    the board.

15. I need _____ see you.
    (point / to)

16. I will go _____ Lisa to
    (with / read)
    the store.

17. Eli likes to _____ on
    (with / work)
    computers.

Foundations of Reading

▶ **Read on Your Own**

Read these sentences.

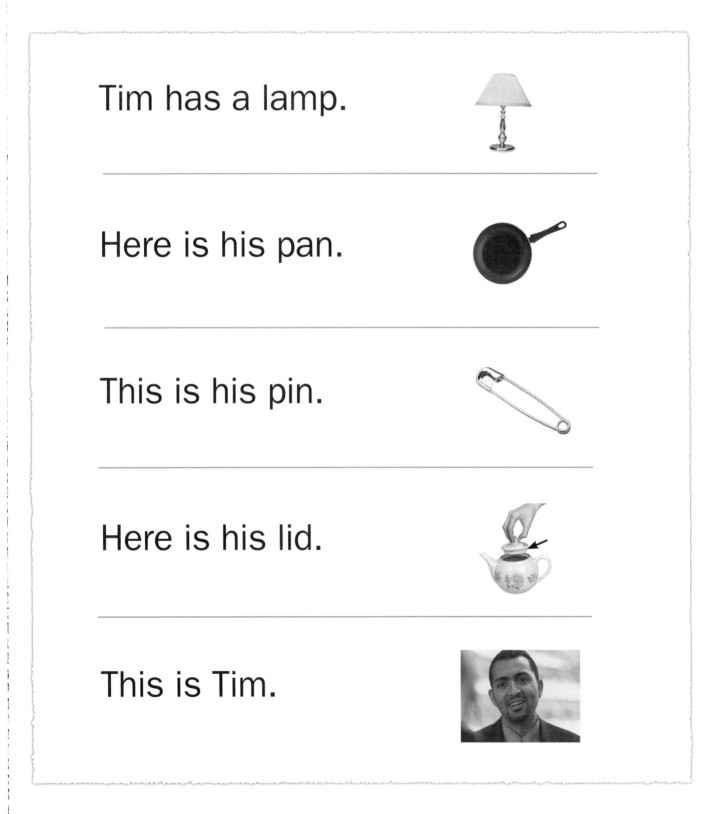

Tim has a lamp.

_____

Here is his pan.

_____

This is his pin.

_____

Here is his lid.

_____

This is Tim.

Foundations of Reading

► Words with Short *a* and *i*

A. Read each word. Draw a line to match the word and the picture.

1.

pan

map

man

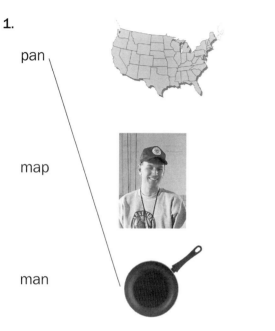

2.

pin

sit

pig

B. Write the missing words.

3.

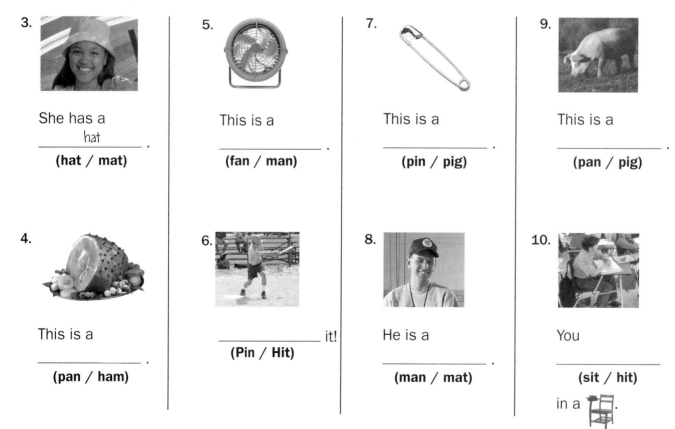

She has a
_____hat_____ .
(hat / mat)

5.

This is a
_____ .
(fan / man)

7.

This is a
_____ .
(pin / pig)

9.

This is a
_____ .
(pan / pig)

4.

This is a
_____ .
(pan / ham)

6.

_____ it!
(Pin / Hit)

8.

He is a
_____ .
(man / mat)

10.

You
_____
(sit / hit)
in a 🪑 .

F16

Foundations of Reading

Name _____

▶ **Words with Short *a* and *i***

A. Write the missing letters. Then read the words in each list. How are the words different?

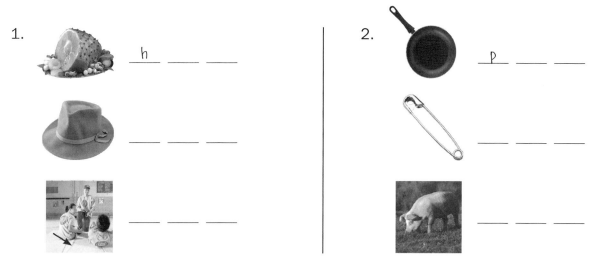

1. h __ __ __

__ __ __

__ __ __

2. p __ __ __

__ __ __

__ __ __

B. Read each question. What word goes in the answer? Spell the word. Then circle the correct picture.

3. Where is the pig?

The __p__ __i__ __g__ is here.

4. Where is the pan?

Here is the __ __ __ .

5. Where is Sam?

__ __ __ is here.

6. Who hit it?

Carlos __ __ __ it.

7. Who has the hat?

She __ __ __ the hat.

8. Who is the man?

He is a __ __ __ .

▶ **Letters and Sounds**

A. Study the new letters and sounds.

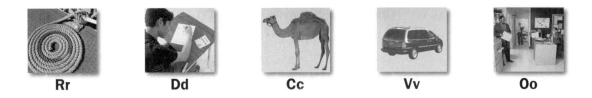

| Rr | Dd | Cc | Vv | Oo |

B. Say the name of each picture below. What letter spells the <u>first</u> sound you hear? Circle the letter.

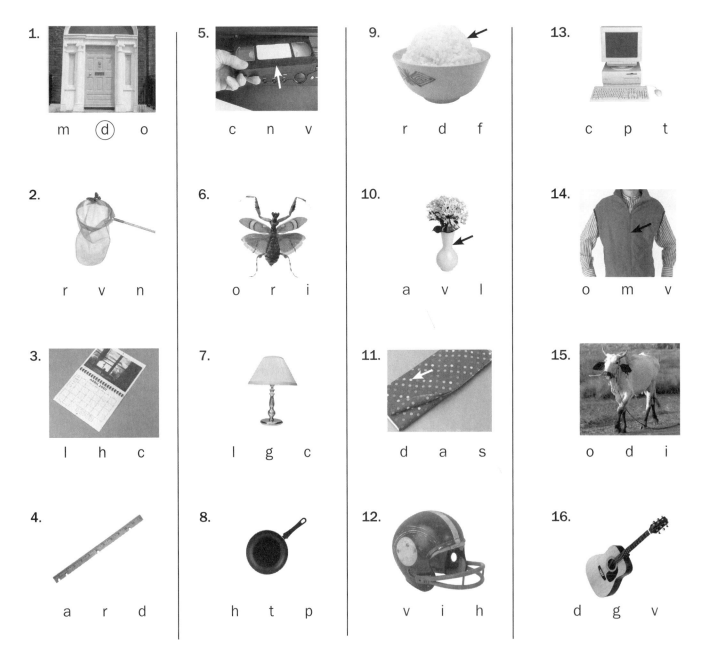

1.   m   (d)   o

5.   c   n   v

9.   r   d   f

13.   c   p   t

2.   r   v   n

6.   o   r   i

10.   a   v   l

14.   o   m   v

3.   l   h   c

7.   l   g   c

11.   d   a   s

15.   o   d   i

4.   a   r   d

8.   h   t   p

12.   v   i   h

16.   d   g   v

Foundations of Reading

► **Letters and Sounds**

Say the name of each picture below. Write the missing letters.

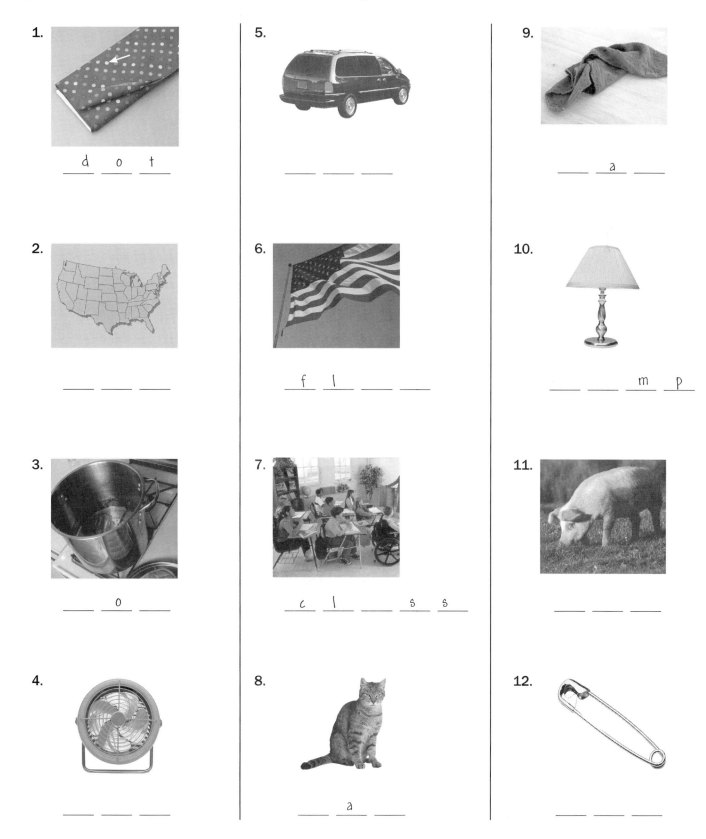

1. __d__ __o__ __t__

2. ___ ___ ___

3. ___ __o__ ___

4. ___ ___ ___

5. ___ ___ ___

6. __f__ __l__ ___ ___

7. __c__ __l__ ___ __s__ __s__

8. ___ __a__ ___

9. ___ __a__ ___

10. ___ ___ __m__ __p__

11. ___ ___ ___

12. ___ ___ ___

▶ **High Frequency Words**

Read each word. Then write it.

1. do _____ 4. help _____

2. does _____ 5. in _____

3. for _____ 6. like _____

How to Play

1. Play with a partner. Each partner chooses a sign. X O

2. Partner 1 reads a word and marks the square with a sign.

3. Partner 2 takes a turn.

4. Get 3 **X**s or **O**s in a row to win.

A.

do	help	like
in	does	for
point	read	to

B.

does	point	read
in	do	help
for	like	to

C.

help	does	do
for	like	in
with	work	write

D.

like	work	does
write	do	help
for	with	in

Foundations of Reading

Name _____

▶ **High Frequency Words**

A. Read each word. Then write it.

1. around _____   4. will _____

2. me _____   5. and _____

3. picture _____   6. don't _____

B. Write the missing letters.

7. Which word has 3 letters?

   a   n   d
  ___   ___   ___

8. Which word is two words together?

  ___ ___ ___ ___

9. Which word has 6 letters?

  ___ ___ ___ ___ ___ ___

10. Which words have an **r**?

  ___ ___ ___ ___ ___

  ___ ___ ___ ___ ___ ___

11. Which word has 2 letters?

  ___ ___

12. Which words have a **d**?

  ___ ___ ___ ___ ___ ___

  ___ ___ ___

  ___ ___ ___

C. Write the missing word.

13. I see your _____ in
             (picture / around)
    the yearbook.

14. Yes, I _____
          (don't / will)
    play basketball.

15. Tell _____ about
        (and / me)
    the game.

16. Can you run _____
        (around / picture)
    the track?

17. Why _____ you
        (don't / and)
    stay there?

Foundations of Reading

Name _____

▶ High Frequency Words

A. Read each word. Then write it.

1. food _____
2. not _____
3. that _____
4. both _____
5. get _____
6. these _____

B. Write the missing letters.

7. Which words have 3 letters?

   n   o   t

   g   e   t

8. Which words have 4 letters?

   ___ ___ ___ ___

   ___ ___ ___ ___

   ___ ___ ___ ___

9. Which words end in **t**?

   ___ ___ ___

   ___ ___ ___

   ___ ___ ___ ___

10. Which words have an **e**?

   ___ ___ ___

   ___ ___ ___ ___ ___

11. Which word has 5 letters?

   ___ ___ ___ ___ ___

C. Write the missing word.

12. I ate the _____ .
    (both / food)

13. Sam saw _____ apple.
    (get / that)

14. I did _____ see the
    (get / not)
    shooting star.

15. Did you _____ help
    (both / food)
    the girl?

16. Did Lin _____ the ball?
    (these / get)

17. We ate _____ chips.
    (food / these)

Name _____

▶ **Read on Your Own**

Read these sentences.

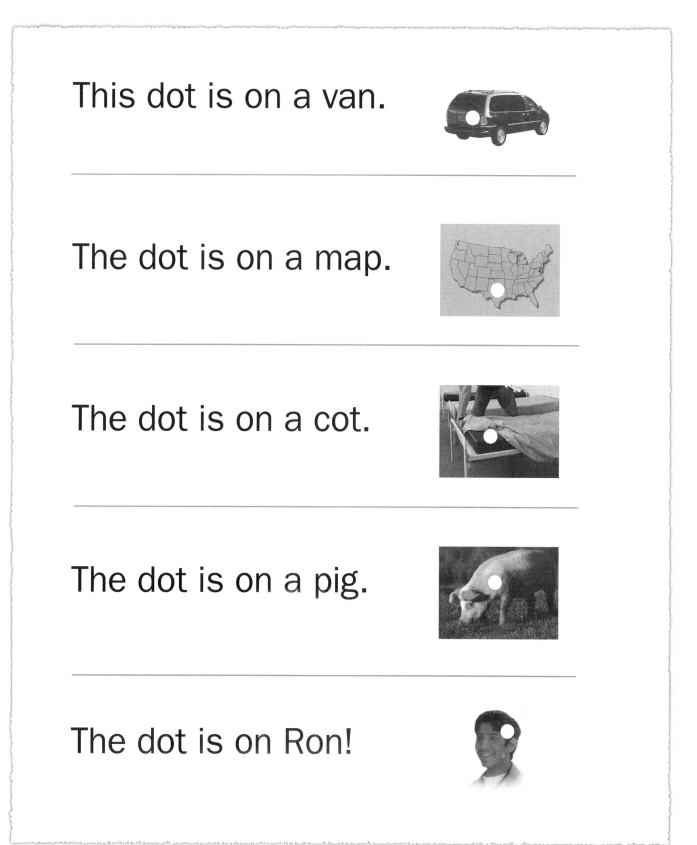

This dot is on a van.

The dot is on a map.

The dot is on a cot.

The dot is on a pig.

The dot is on Ron!

Foundations of Reading

Name _____

▶ **Words with Short *a*, *i*, and *o***

A. Read each word. Draw a line to the correct picture.

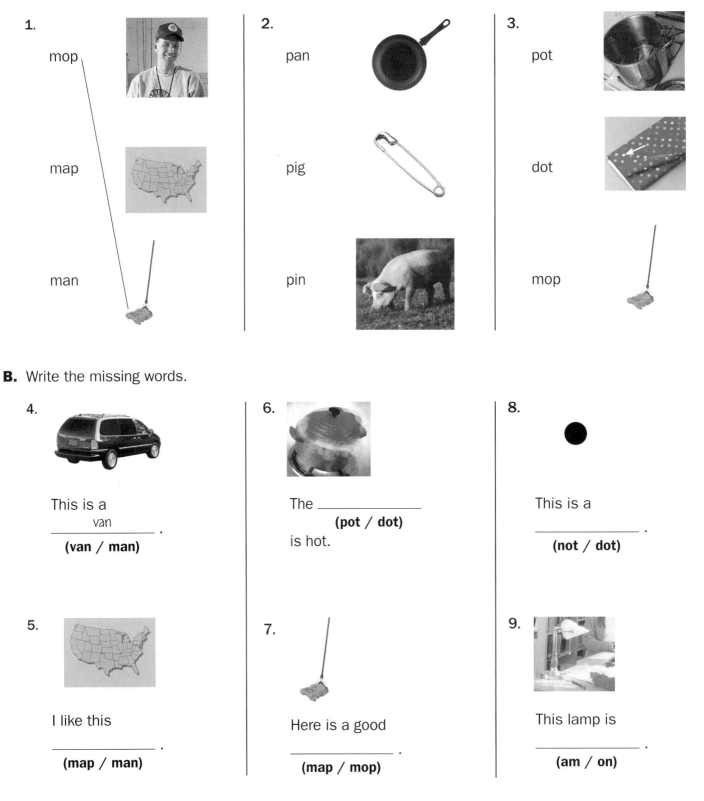

1.
mop
map
man

2.
pan
pig
pin

3.
pot
dot
mop

B. Write the missing words.

4.
This is a
___van___ .
(van / man)

5.
I like this
_____ .
(map / man)

6.
The _____
(pot / dot)
is hot.

7.
Here is a good
_____ .
(map / mop)

8.
This is a
_____ .
(not / dot)

9.
This lamp is
_____ .
(am / on)

Foundations of Reading

▶ Words with Short *a*, *i*, and *o*

A. Write the missing letters. Then read the words in each list. How are the words different?

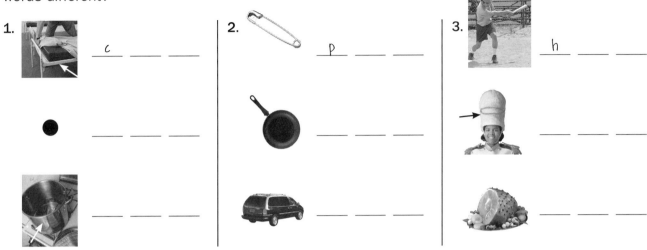

1. _c_ _ _ _

   _ _ _ _

   _ _ _ _

2. _p_ _ _ _

   _ _ _ _

   _ _ _ _

3. _h_ _ _ _

   _ _ _ _

   _ _ _ _

B. Read each question and the answer. Write the missing words. Then circle the correct picture.

4. Is this pot hot?

   No, the _p_ _o_ _t_ is not _h_ _o_ _t_.

7. Where can I sit?

   You can ____ ____ ____ here.

5. Is this your cap?

   Yes, it is my ____ ____ ____ .

8. Point to the dot.

   The ____ ____ ____ is here!

6. Where is the mop?

   The ____ ____ ____ is here.

9. Do you like the hat?

   Yes, I like the ____ ____ ____ .

Foundations of Reading

Name _____

▶ Letters and Sounds

Study the new letters and sounds.

| Jj | Bb | Ww | Kk | Ee |

How to Play Bingo

1. Write the letters from the box. Write one letter in each square.

2. Then listen to the word your teacher reads.

3. Put a ◯ on the letter that stands for the first sound in the word.

4. The first player to cover all the letters in a row is the winner.

Letters to Write

a	i	p
b	j	r
b	j	s
c	k	t
d	k	v
e	l	w
f	m	w
g	n	
h	o	

Words to Read

am	got	lot	top
bat	hit	mat	van
big	it	not	win
can	jam	on	wig
dot	jog	pin	
egg	kid	red	
fat	kit	sit	

Foundations of Reading

Name _____

▶ Letters and Sounds

Say the name of each picture below. Write the missing letters.

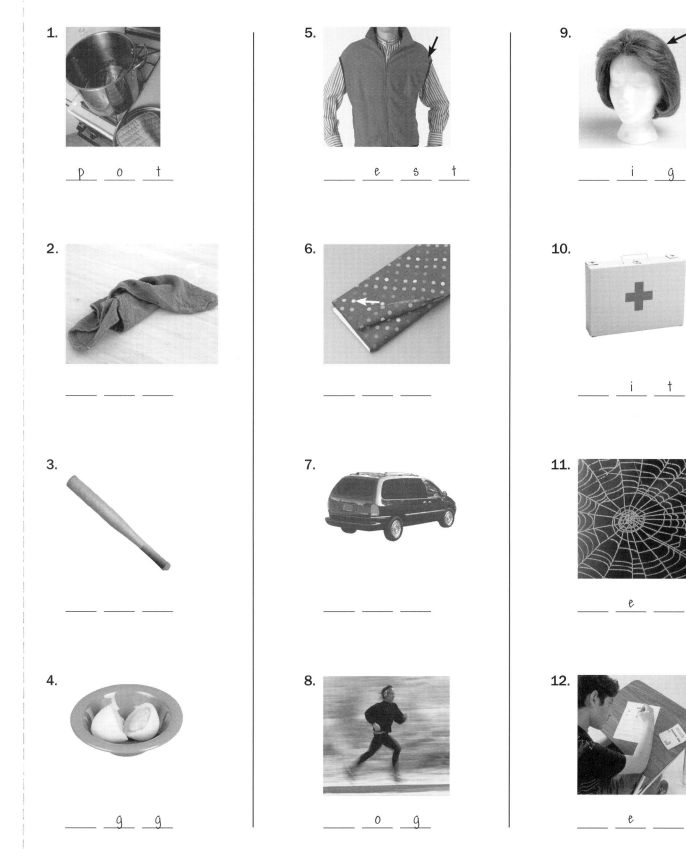

1. __p__ __o__ __t__

2. ___ ___ ___

3. ___ ___ ___

4. ___ __g__ __g__

5. ___ __e__ __s__ __t__

6. ___ ___ ___

7. ___ ___ ___

8. ___ __o__ __g__

9. ___ __i__ __g__

10. ___ __i__ __t__

11. ___ __e__ ___

12. ___ __e__ ___

Foundations of Reading

Name _____

▶ **High Frequency Words**

A. Read each word. Then write it.

1. things	_____	4. them	_____
2. little	_____	5. those	_____
3. old	_____	6. very	_____

B. Write the missing letters.

7. Which word has 3 letters?

   o   l   d
___ ___ ___

8. Which words have an **i**?

___ ___ ___ ___ ___ ___

___ ___ ___ ___ ___ ___

9. Which word has a **v**?

___ ___ ___ ___

10. Which words have 4 letters?

___ ___ ___ ___

___ ___ ___ ___

C. Write the missing word.

11. The food is _____ good.
          (very / little)

12. Did you see _____
         (things / those)
bananas?

13. The flea was very _____ .
         (them / little)

14. I saw _____ at school.
       (them / very)

15. The _____ dog liked
     (things / old)
to sleep.

16. I have many _____ .
        (those / things)

Foundations of Reading

▶ **High Frequency Words**

A. Read each word. Then write it.

1. think _____   4. which _____

2. take _____   5. can _____

3. give _____   6. play _____

B. Write the missing letters.

7. Which words have 4 letters?

t   a   k   e
___ ___ ___ ___

___ ___ ___ ___

___ ___ ___ ___

8. Which words have 5 letters?

___ ___ ___ ___ ___

___ ___ ___ ___ ___

9. Which word has a **g**?

___ ___ ___ ___

10. Which word has 3 letters?

___ ___ ___

11. Which words have an **a**?

___ ___ ___

___ ___ ___

___ ___ ___ ___

C. Write the missing word.

12. I _____ I know the
    (think / play)
    answer.

13. Juan _____ run very fast.
    (which / can)

14. _____ your turn next.
    (Take / Which)

15. Can you _____ baseball?
    (can / play)

16. _____ book is yours?
    (Take / Which)

17. Let's _____ food to the
    (give / play)
    hamster.

Foundations of Reading

▶ High Frequency Words

A. Read each word. Then write it.

1. too _____   4. have _____

2. feel _____   5. how _____

3. has _____   6. put _____

B. Write the missing letters.

7. Which words have 3 letters?

t o o
___ ___ ___

___ ___ ___

___ ___ ___

___ ___ ___

8. Which words have 4 letters?

___ ___ ___ ___

___ ___ ___ ___

9. Which words have an **h**?

___ ___ ___

___ ___ ___

___ ___ ___ ___

10. Which word ends with a **t**?

___ ___ ___

11. Which word has two **e**'s?

___ ___ ___ ___

C. Write the missing word.

12. She has brown hair, _____ .
    (too / how)

13. Where did you _____
    (how / put)
    the book?

14. Do you _____ sick today?
    (have / feel)

15. She _____ a blue
    (has / have)
    backpack.

16. _____ are you feeling
    (Have / How)
    today?

17. I _____ two cookies.
    (how / have)

Foundations of Reading

Name _____

▶ **Read on Your Own**

Read these sentences.

Can Ken jog?

Ken can jog well.

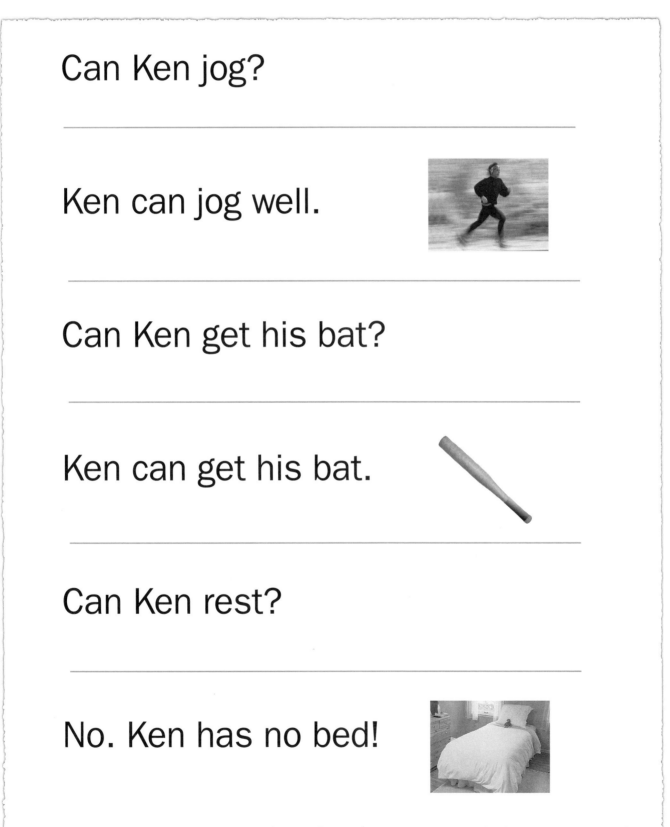

Can Ken get his bat?

Ken can get his bat.

Can Ken rest?

No. Ken has no bed!

Foundations of Reading

▶ Words with Short *a*, *i*, *o*, and *e*

A. Read each word. Draw a line to the correct picture.

1.
jam

ham

hat
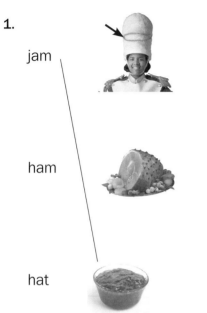

2.
pen

ten

men
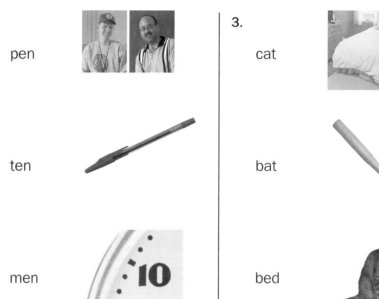

3.
cat

bat

bed

B. Write the missing words.

4.
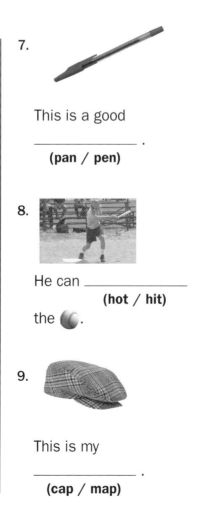
Here are two

___men___ .

(men / ten)

7.
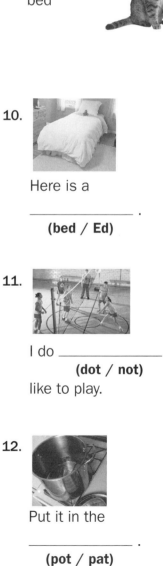
This is a good

_____ .

(pan / pen)

10.
Here is a

_____ .

(bed / Ed)

5. ● ● ● ● ●
   ● ● ● ● ●

There are

_____ dots.

(ten / pen)

8.

He can _____
         (hot / hit)

the 🔴.

11.

I do _____
      (dot / not)
like to play.

6.
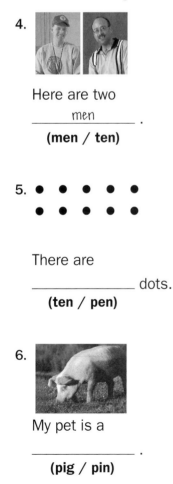
My pet is a

_____ .

(pig / pin)

9.

This is my

_____ .

(cap / map)

12.

Put it in the

_____ .

(pot / pat)

Foundations of Reading

Name _____

► Words with Short *a*, *i*, *o*, and *e*

A. Write the missing letters. Then read the words in each list. How are the words different?

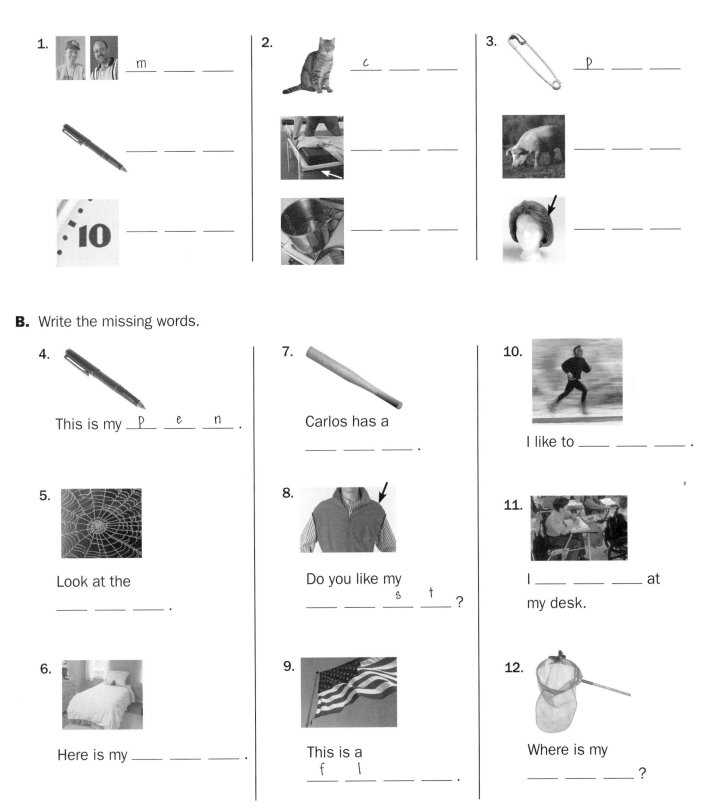

1. m __ __ __

    __ __ __

    __ __ __

2. c __ __ __

    __ __ __

    __ __ __

3. p __ __ __

    __ __ __

    __ __ __

B. Write the missing words.

4. This is my p e n .

5. Look at the __ __ __ .

6. Here is my __ __ __ .

7. Carlos has a __ __ __ .

8. Do you like my __ __ s __ t ?

9. This is a f l __ __ .

10. I like to __ __ __ .

11. I __ __ __ at my desk.

12. Where is my __ __ __ ?

Foundations of Reading

▶ Letters and Sounds

Study the new letters and sounds.

| Zz | Yy | Uu | Qq | Xx |

How to Play Bingo

1. Write the letters from the box. Write one letter in each square.

2. Then listen to the word your teacher reads.

3. Put a ◯ on the letter that stands for the first sound in the word.

4. The first player to cover all the letters in a row is the winner.

Letters to Write

a	j	s
b	k	t
c	l	u
d	m	v
e	n	w
f	o	y
g	p	z
h	q	
i	r	

Words to Read

am	him	on	van
bat	in	pen	wig
cot	jam	quit	yes
dot	kid	red	zip
egg	lot	sat	
fan	map	ten	
got	not	up	

Foundations of Reading

Name _____

▶ Letters and Sounds

Say the name of each picture below. Write the missing letters.

1.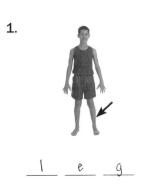

l   e   g

2.

___   ___   i   l   t

3.

___   ___

4.

___   ___   ___

5.

___   ___   ___

6.

___   ___   ___   ___

7.

___   u   ___

8.

___   u   ___

9.

___   ___   ___

10.

___   ___   ___

11.

___   u   ___

12.

___   ___   ___

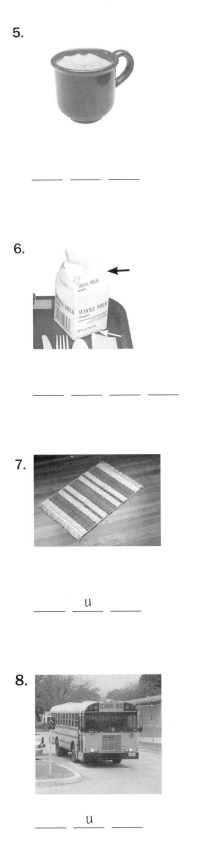

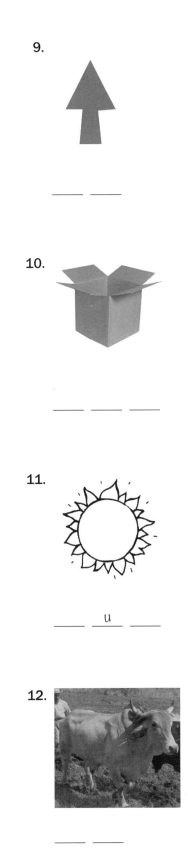

Foundations of Reading

Name _____

▶ High Frequency Words

A. Read each word. Then write it.

1. they	_____	4. soon	_____
2. great	_____	5. tomorrow	_____
3. later	_____	6. call	_____

B. Write the missing letters.

7. Which words have 4 letters?

t   h   e   y
__ __ __ __

__ __ __ __

__ __ __ __

8. Which words have 5 letters?

__ __ __ __ __

__ __ __ __ __

9. Which words have an **a**?

__ __ __ __ __

__ __ __ __ __

__ __ __ __

10. Which word ends with a **t**?

__ __ __ __ __

11. Which word has 8 letters?

__ __ __ __ __ __ __ __

C. Write the missing word.

12. I will be in class _____ .
    (great / tomorrow)

13. I will see him _____ ,
    (soon / they)
    I hope!

14. Shana will be there _____ .
    (later / call)

15. Did you _____ your
    (call / soon)
    dad yet?

16. He did _____ on the test.
    (soon / great)

17. When will _____ be here?
    (they / call)

Foundations of Reading

▶ High Frequency Words

A. Read each word. Then write it.

1. name _____
2. need _____
3. number _____

4. we _____
5. what _____
6. book _____

B. Write the missing letters.

7. Which word has 2 letters?

w   e
___ ___

8. Which words have 4 letters?

___ ___ ___ ___

___ ___ ___ ___

___ ___ ___ ___

___ ___ ___ ___

9. Which word has 6 letters?

___ ___ ___ ___ ___ ___

10. Which word ends with a **t**?

___ ___ ___ ___

11. Which word has an **r**?

___ ___ ___ ___ ___ ___

C. Write the missing word.

12. What is your _____ ?
   (we / name)

13. Find the _____ ten.
   (number / book)

14. The _____ is on the shelf.
   (book / need)

15. _____ went to the library.
   (We / Number)

16. I _____ to do my
   (need / what)
   homework.

17. _____ did you do last
   (What / We)
   week?

Name _____

▶ **High Frequency Words**

A. Read each word. Then write it.

1. boy _____ 4. group _____

2. day _____ 5. letters _____

3. girl _____ 6. night _____

7. year _____

B. Write the missing letters.

8. Which word ends with a **p**?

<u>g</u> <u>r</u> <u>o</u> <u>u</u> <u>p</u>

9. Which words have 3 letters?

___ ___ ___

___ ___ ___

10. Which words have 5 letters?

___ ___ ___ ___ ___

___ ___ ___ ___ ___

11. Which word ends with **s**?

___ ___ ___ ___ ___ ___ ___

12. Which words have a **y** in them?

___ ___ ___ ___

___ ___ ___

___ ___ ___

C. Write the missing word.

13. I saw the _____ in class.
    (night / boy)

14. Last _____, the sky
    (group / night)
    was clear.

15. He has many _____
    (letters / day)
    from Tom.

16. During the _____ the sun
    (day / night)
    is out.

17. The _____ plays basketball.
    (year / girl)

18. There is a _____
    (boy / group)
    of students.

19. This _____ I am a freshman.
    (night / year)

▶ **Read on Your Own**

Read these sentences.

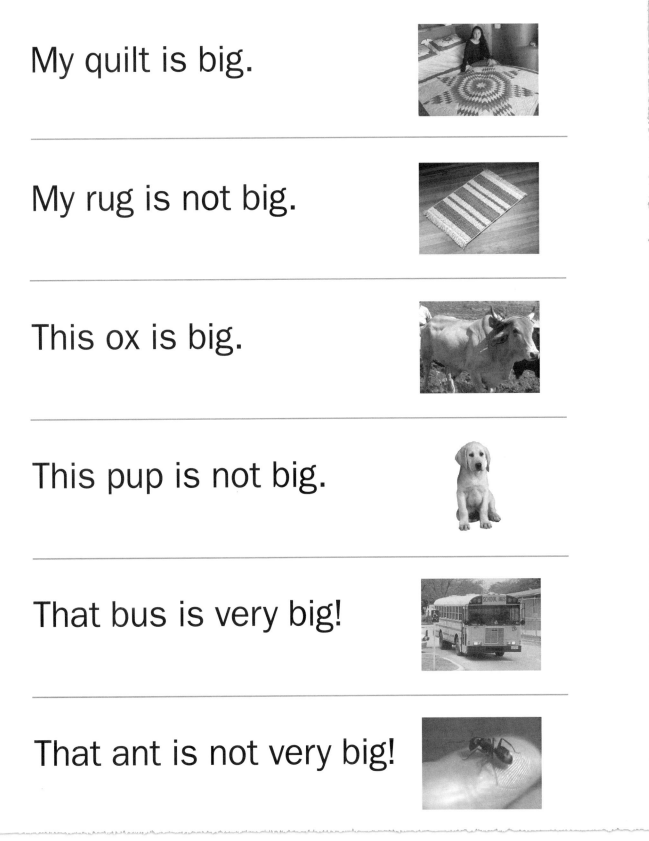

My quilt is big.

My rug is not big.

This ox is big.

This pup is not big.

That bus is very big!

That ant is not very big!

Foundations of Reading

▶ Words with Short *a*, *i*, *o*, *e*, and *u*

A. Read each word. Draw a line to the correct picture.

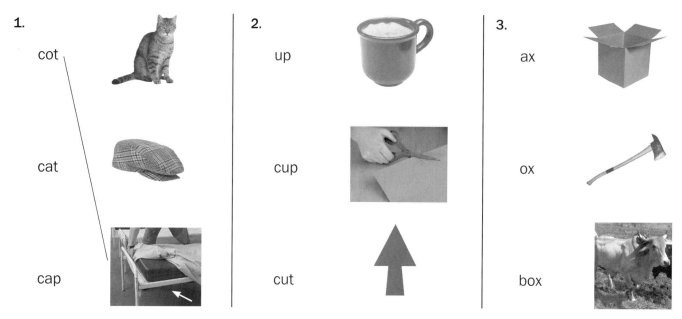

1.
cot
cat
cap

2.
up
cup
cut

3.
ax
ox
box

B. Say the name of each picture below. Write the missing letters.

4.

I can __z__ __i__ __p__ it.

6.

I like this old

___ ___ ___ ___ ___ .

8.

I have ___ ___ ___

pins.

5.

This is my ___ ___ ___ .

7.

Do you like my little

___ ___ ___ ?

9.

Is this a pig?

___ ___ ___ !

Foundations of Reading

Name _____

▶ **Words with Short *a, i, o, e,* and *u***

A. Write the missing letters. Then read the words in each list. How are the words different?

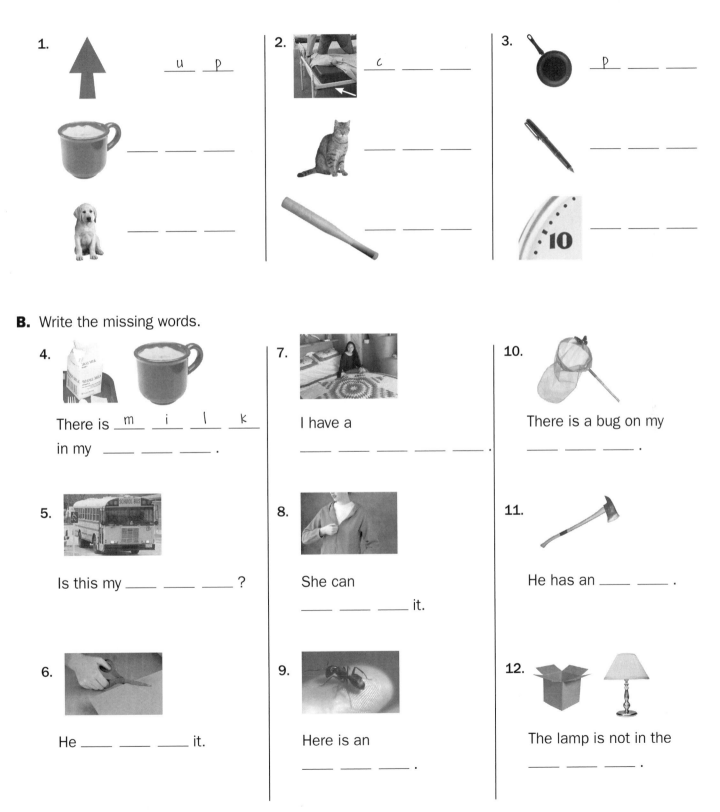

1. u p

2. c ___ ___

3. p ___ ___

B. Write the missing words.

4. There is __m__ __i__ __l__ __k__ in my ___ ___ ___ .

5. Is this my ___ ___ ___ ?

6. He ___ ___ ___ it.

7. I have a ___ ___ ___ ___ .

8. She can ___ ___ ___ it.

9. Here is an ___ ___ ___ .

10. There is a bug on my ___ ___ ___ .

11. He has an ___ ___ .

12. The lamp is not in the ___ ___ ___ .

Reading Practice

High Frequency Words, Part 1

A. Read each word. Then write it.

1. from   _____

2. home   _____

3. new   _____

4. go   _____

5. there   _____

B. Read each sentence. Find the new words in the box. Write the words on the lines.

6. These two words have an **m**.

   _____from_____   _____

7. This word has 3 letters.

   _____

8. This word is the opposite of **stop**.

   _____

9. This word rhymes with **where**.

   _____

10. This word starts with **fr**.

    _____

High Frequency Words, Part 2

A. Read each word. Then write it.

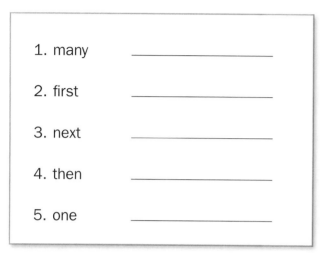

1. many _____

2. first _____

3. next _____

4. then _____

5. one _____

B. Read each sentence. Find the new words in the box. Write the words on the lines.

6. This word has an **m**.

   _____many_____

7. These 3 words tell "when."

   _____   _____   _____

8. This word has 3 letters.

   _____

9. These 3 words have 4 letters each.

   _____   _____   _____

10. This word has an **o**.

    _____

Reading Practice

Words with Short *a* and Short *o*

A. Name each picture. Write the name.

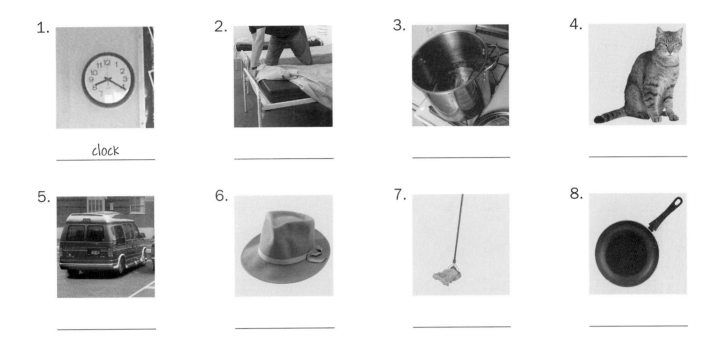

1. clock
2. _____
3. _____
4. _____

5. _____
6. _____
7. _____
8. _____

B. Now read the story. Circle the words with short *a* or short *o*. Write them in the chart. Write each word one time.

(Cat) Fun

Sam has a cat.

The cat has lots of fun.

It hops on the hat.

It naps in a pot.

It got into a pan.

It sleeps on the van.

When the cat is hot,

It jumps on the cot.

The cat can be bad.

But Sam likes his cat!

9. cat	18. _____
10. _____	19. _____
11. _____	20. _____
12. _____	21. _____
13. _____	22. _____
14. _____	23. _____
15. _____	24. _____
16. _____	
17. _____	

Reading Practice

Words with Short *a* and Short *o*

A. Name each picture. Write the name.

1.

_____hat_____

2.

_____

3.

_____

4.

_____

5.

_____

6.

_____

7.

_____

8.

_____

B. Now read the story. Circle the words with short *a* or short *o*. Write them in the chart. Write each word one time.

I See a (Van)

I see a van.

It has a lot of things in it!

I see a map and a box in the van.

I see a mop and a fan in the van.

I see some pots and pans, too.

Is Tom in the van?

Tom is not in the van. There is no room!

9. _____van_____	15. _____
10. _____	16. _____
11. _____	17. _____
12. _____	18. _____
13. _____	19. _____
14. _____	20. _____

Reading Practice

Words with Short *a* and Short *o*

A. Read each word. Which picture goes with the word? Write its letter.

1. fan   _B_
2. box   ___
3. cap   ___
4. flag   ___
5. apple   ___

6. dot   ___
7. rock   ___
8. bat   ___
9. jog   ___
10. tag   ___

11. map   ___
12. spots   ___
13. ox   ___
14. cloth   ___
15. frog   ___

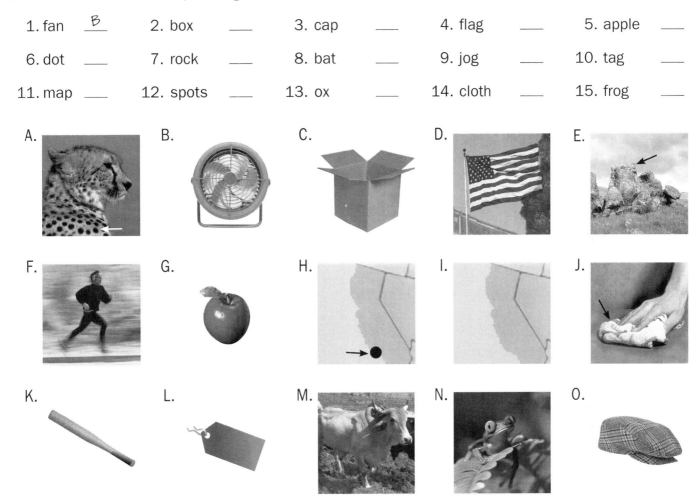

A.   B.   C.   D.   E.

F.   G.   H.   I.   J.

K.   L.   M.   N.   O.

B. Name each picture below. Which word or words above rhyme with the picture name? Write the words on the lines.

16. _flag_ ___

17. ___ ___

18. ___

Reading Practice

Words with Short *a* and Short *o*

A. Read each word. Which picture goes with the word? Write its letter.

1. cot *G*
2. cap ___
3. fan ___
4. top ___
5. jog ___

6. bag ___
7. fog ___
8. dot ___
9. van ___
10. rag ___

11. hop ___
12. bat ___
13. nap ___
14. hat ___
15. sad ___

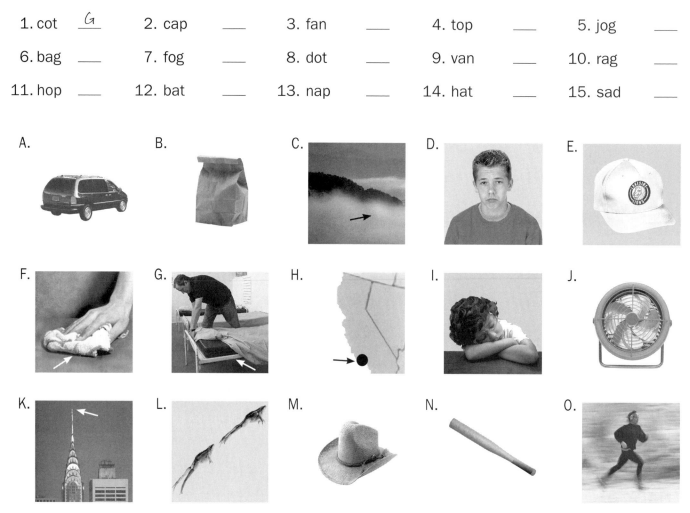

A. B. C. D. E.

F. G. H. I. J.

K. L. M. N. O.

B. Read each word. Find the word or words above that have the same vowel sound and spelling. Write the words on the lines.

16. _____ *cap* _____

17. _____

18. _____

19. _____

20. _____

21. _____

22. _____

23. _____

Name _____

High Frequency Words, Part 1

A. Read each word. Then write it.

1. something _____

2. make _____

3. long _____

4. large _____

5. move _____

B. Read the clue. Write the word in the chart. Then write the word again in the sentence.

What to Look For	Word	Sentence
6. has the word **some** in it	s o m e t h i n g	I want _something_ hot.
7. rhymes with **take**	__ __ __ __	You _____ great food.
8. rhymes with **song**	__ __ __ __	I like _____ noodles.
9. means "big"	__ __ __ __ __	You have a _____ bag.
10. ends with **ve**	__ __ __ __	Please _____ over.

Name _____

High Frequency Words, Part 2

A. Read each word. Then write it.

1. different   _____

2. small   _____

3. open   _____

4. same   _____

5. eat   _____

B. Read the clue. Write the word in the chart. Then write the word again in the sentence.

What to Look For	Word	Sentence
6. has **ff**	d i f f e r e n t	Your bag is ___different___ .
7. starts with **sm**	__ __ __ __ __	My lunch is in a _____ bag.
8. starts with **o**	__ __ __ __	I _____ my lunch bag.
9. ends with **me**	__ __ __ __	Our food is not the _____ .
10. has three letters	__ __ __	It is time to _____ .

Reading Practice

Name _____

Words with Short *i* and Short *u*

A. Name each picture. Write the name.

1.

pig

2.

_____

3.

_____

4.

_____

5.

_____

6.

_____

7.

_____

8.

_____

B. Now read the story. Circle the words with short *i* or short *u*. Write them in the chart. Write each word one time.

My New (Pup)

Yesterday I got a new pup.
She sips milk from a little cup.
We sit in the sun.
Then we go for a run.
I know one day my pup will get big.
I pray she never looks like a pig!
For now I just love my silly mutt.

9. _____	15. _____pup_____
10. _____	16. _____
11. _____	17. _____
12. _____	18. _____
13. _____	19. _____
14. _____	20. _____
	21. _____
	22. _____
	23. _____

Name _____

Words with Short *i* and Short *u*

A. Name each picture. Write the name.

1.

_____pin_____

2.

_____

3.

_____

4.

_____

5.

_____

6.

_____

7.

_____

8.

_____

B. Now read the story. Circle the words with short *i* or short *u*. Write them in the chart. Write each word one time.

(Just) Great!

Sam needs something to eat.
He rips open a bag of chips.
The chips are good, but not great.
Sam cuts a bit of ham and
slaps it on a bun.
The ham is good, but not great.
Mom comes in.
She gets a cup of ice cream.
She adds lots of nuts.
Sam grins. Yes! That is great!

9. ____Just____	15. _____
10. _____	16. _____
11. _____	17. _____
12. _____	18. _____
13. _____	19. _____
14. _____	20. _____
	21. _____

Words with Short *i* and Short *u*

A. Read each word. Which picture goes with the word? Write its letter.

1. cup _G_   2. fin ___   3. pump ___   4. hit ___   5. sit ___

6. rug ___   7. disk ___   8. nut ___   9. pig ___   10. dig ___

11. sun ___   12. pin ___   13. cut ___   14. lid ___   15. bun ___

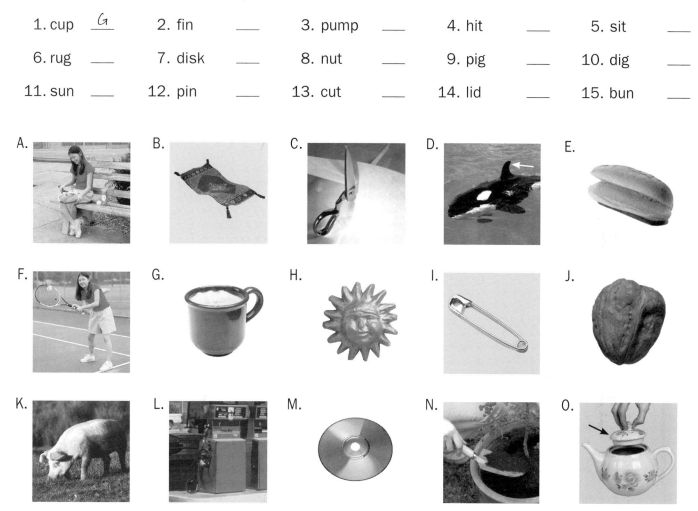

B. Name each picture below. Which word or words above rhyme with the picture name? Write the words on the lines.

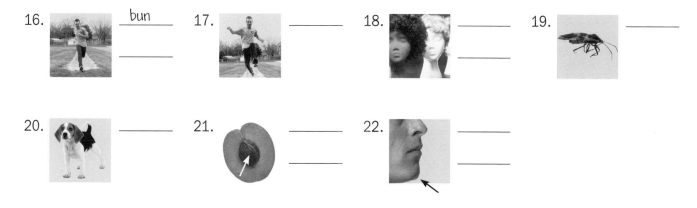

16. bun   17. ___   18. ___   19. ___

20. ___   21. ___   22. ___

Reading Practice

Name _____

Words with Short *i* and Short *u*

A. Write the missing letters. Then read the words in each list. How are the words different?

1.
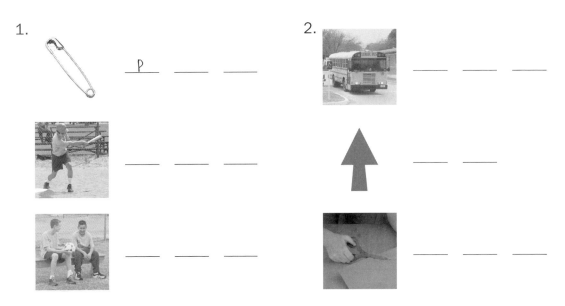
p _____ _____ _____

_____ _____ _____

_____ _____ _____

2.
_____ _____ _____

_____ _____ _____

_____ _____ _____

B. Read each question. What word goes in the answer? Spell the word. Then circle the correct picture.

3. Where is the cup? The __c__ _____ _____ is here.

4. Who made a hit? John made a

_____ _____ _____ .

5. Where is the first-aid kit? The first-aid

_____ _____ _____ is here.

6. Where is the pup? The _____ _____ _____ is here.

7. Who can zip it? The girl can

_____ _____ _____ it.

8. Where is the fish? Here is the

_____ _____ _____ _____ .

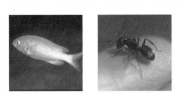

Name _____

High Frequency Words, Part 1

A. Read each word. Then write it.

1. study _____

2. learn _____

3. carry _____

4. find _____

5. use _____

B. Read each sentence. Find the new words in the box. Write the words on the lines.

6. This word starts with **st**.

_____ study _____

7. This word starts with **l**.

_____

8. These 3 words have 5 letters each.

_____ _____ _____

9. This word has an **i**.

_____

10. This word ends with **e**.

_____

High Frequency Words, Part 2

A. Read each word. Then write it.

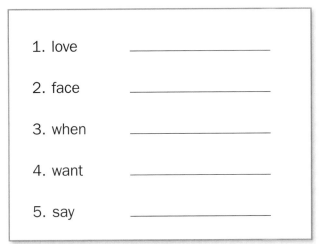

1. love _____

2. face _____

3. when _____

4. want _____

5. say _____

B. Read each sentence. Find the new words in the box. Write the words on the lines.

6. This word starts with **l**.

_____ love _____

7. These 2 words end with **e**.

_____   _____

8. This word rhymes with **then**.

_____

9. This word ends with **nt**.

_____

10. This word rhymes with **day**.

_____

Name _____

Words with Short e

A. Read each word. Which picture goes with the word? Write its letter.

1. web __G__   2. fence ____   3. bell ____

4. desk ____   5. ten ____   6. hen ____

7. egg ____   8. vest ____   9. leg ____

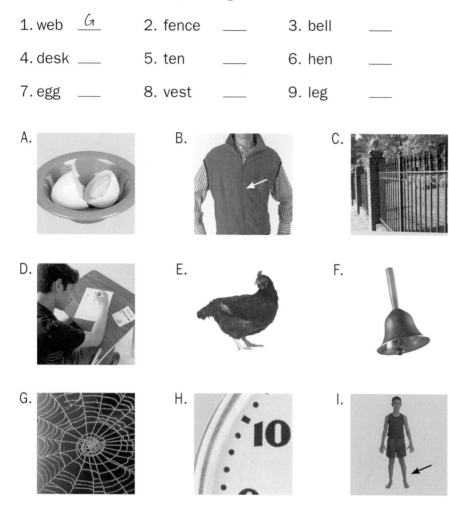

A.   B.   C.

D.   E.   F.

G.   H.   I.

B. Read each sentence. Write the correct word on the line.

10. This word rhymes with **best**.

_____

11. This word rhymes with **tell**.

_____

Words with Short e

A. Read each word. Which picture goes with the word? Write its letter.

1. hen _F_   2. check ___   3. net ___   4. pet ___

5. bed ___   6. chest ___   7. pen ___   8. vet ___

9. egg ___   10. bench ___   11. stretch ___   12. send ___

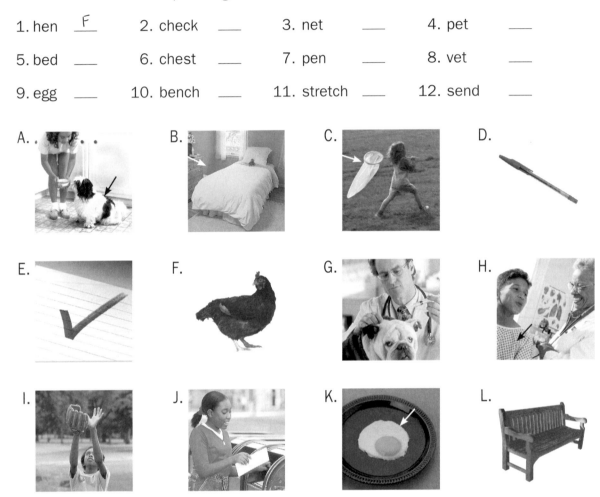

A.   B.   C.   D.

E.   F.   G.   H.

I.   J.   K.   L.

B. Name each picture below. Which words above rhyme with the picture name? Write the words on the lines.

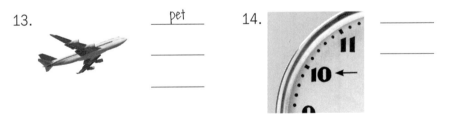

13.   ___pet___

14.   _____

Reading Practice

Final *ll, ss, zz, ck*

A. Read each word. Which picture goes with the word? Write its letter.

1. chick ___A___ 2. pill ___ 3. bell ___ 4. fizz ___

5. check ___ 6. jazz ___ 7. kiss ___ 8. spill ___

9. rock ___ 10. sick ___ 11. dress ___ 12. hill ___

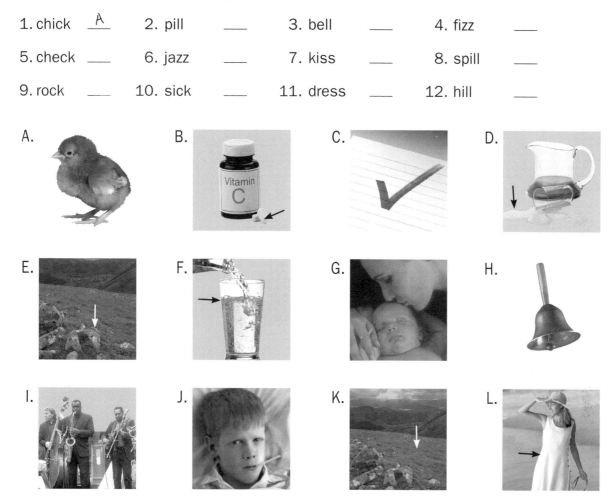

A. B. C. D.

E. F. G. H.

I. J. K. L.

B. Name each picture below. What is the last sound? Find the words above that have the same sound at the end. Write the words on the lines.

13.    ___pill___

___

___

___

14. 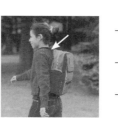   ___

___

___

___

Reading Practice

Words with *sh*

A. Read each word. Which picture goes with the word? Write its letter.

1. shirt *B*
2. fish ___
3. trash ___
4. ship ___
5. shell ___
6. shoulder ___

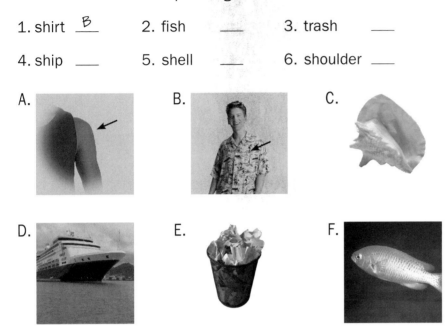

A. B. C.

D. E. F.

B. Now read the story. Circle the words with the *sh* sound. Write the words in the chart. Write each word one time.

(Shiny) New Shoes

I have a pair of shiny new shoes. They are

a pale shade of blue. I think the shoelaces

are too short. After school, I will take them

back to the shop. I will show the laces to the

salesman. I will not be shy. Tonight I will put

my new shoes on a shelf. I will shut the door

and go to sleep.

7. _shiny_	12. _____
8. _____	13. _____
9. _____	14. _____
10. _____	15. _____
11. _____	16. _____

Name _____

High Frequency Words, Part 1

A. Read each word. Then write it.

1. leave   _____

2. two   _____

3. out   _____

4. three   _____

5. all   _____

B. Work with a partner. Follow the steps.

- Read aloud each new word in the box.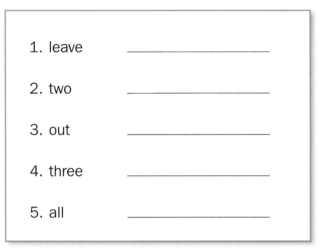

- Your partner writes the words.

- Have your partner read the words to you.

- Now you write the words on the lines below.

- Read the words to your partner.

6. _____

7. _____

8. _____

9. _____

10. _____

High Frequency Words, Part 2

A. Read each word. Then write it.

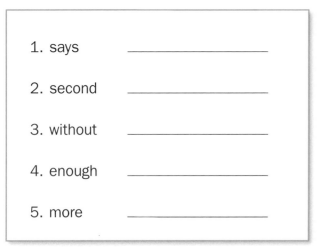

1. says   _____

2. second   _____

3. without   _____

4. enough   _____

5. more   _____

B. Find the new words in the box. Write the words on the lines.

6. These 2 words begin with **s**.

_____says_____   _____

C. Work with a partner. Follow the steps.

• Read aloud each new word in the box.

• Your partner writes the words.

• Have your partner read the words to you.

• Now you write the words on the lines below.

• Read the words to your partner.

7. _____

8. _____

9. _____

10. _____

11. _____

Reading Practice

Words with Digraphs

A. Name each picture. Write the name.

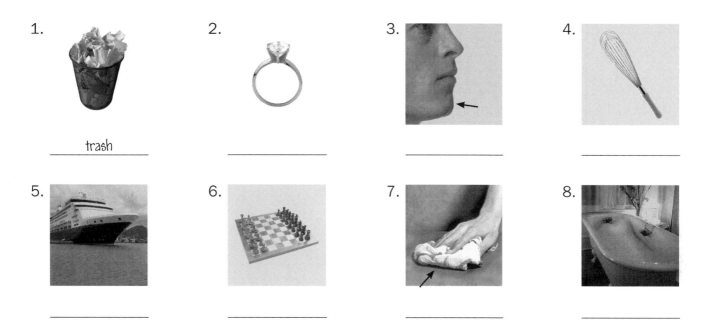

1. _____trash_____

2. _____

3. _____

4. _____

5. _____

6. _____

7. _____

8. _____

B. Now read the story. Circle the words that go in the chart. Write them in the chart. Write each word one time.

A Trip to (the) (Shop)

Dad and I go out to a shop. I think it sells great shells. We can bring some to Mom. I pick six shells and Dad pays cash. There is one more thing we want to do – find some fresh fish to eat. When we go home, Dad gives Mom the shells. Mom loves them and puts them on a shelf. What a great day!

Starts with *th*	Starts with *sh*
9. _____the_____	16. _____Shop_____
10. _____	17. _____
11. _____	18. _____
12. _____	
13. _____	

Ends with *ng*	Ends with *sh*
14. _____	19. _____
15. _____	20. _____
	21. _____

Reading Practice

Words with Blends and Digraphs

A. Name each picture. Write the name.

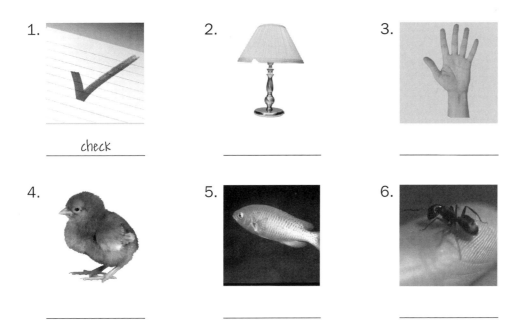

1. _____
   check

2. _____

3. _____

4. _____

5. _____

6. _____

B. Now read the story. Circle the words that go in the chart. Write them in the chart. Write each word one time.

Sal's Big (Trunk)

Sal has a big trunk. He fills it with things.

Open the trunk and look in. You will see five

clocks, sixteen red caps, a brush for a cat, and

ten tops. You will see a chess set, a little lamp,

a belt, twenty rocks, and bath stuff.

Do you like Sal's trunk? We can shut the

trunk now.

Starts with *tr*	Ends with *mp*
7. _____ trunk _____	11. _____
Starts with *cl*	**Ends with *lt***
8. _____	12. _____
Starts with *sh*	**Ends with *sh***
9. _____	13. _____
Starts with *ch*	**Ends with *th***
10. _____	14. _____

Reading Practice

Words with Blends

A. Name each picture. Write the name.

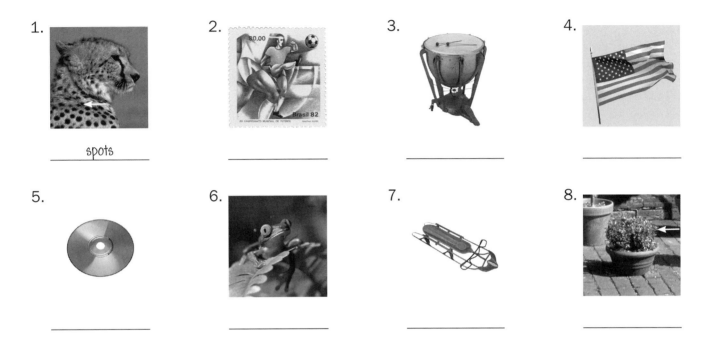

1. _____spots_____

2. _____

3. _____

4. _____

5. _____

6. _____

7. _____

8. _____

B. Now read the story. Circle the words that go in the chart. Write them in the chart. Write each word one time.

Pack for (Camp)

Jim packs his bag for camp. He needs enough

stuff to last 5 days.

He packs:

- 1 tent and a mat to sleep on

- 2 swim trunks for his swim class

- a belt, 4 snacks, 10 socks, 1 brush,

  and more!

He can smash it all in the bag, but he can not

lift the bag! Jim has to pack two bags for camp.

Starts with *st*	Ends with *st*
9. _____	13. _____
Starts with *tr*	**Ends with *nt***
10. _____	14. _____
Starts with *cl*	**Ends with *mp***
11. _____	15. _____Camp_____
Starts with *sn*	**Ends with *lt***
12. _____	16. _____

High Frequency Words, Part 1

A. Read each word. Then write it.

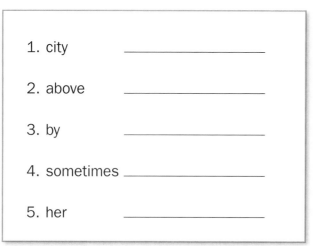

1. city _____

2. above _____

3. by _____

4. sometimes _____

5. her _____

B. Read each sentence. Find the new words in the box. Write the words on the lines.

6. These 2 words end with **y**.

_____city_____   _____

7. These 2 words are location words.

_____   _____

8. This word rhymes with **my**.

_____

9. This word has 2 smaller words in it.

_____

10. This word has **er**.

_____

Name _____

High Frequency Words, Part 2

A. Read each word. Then write it.

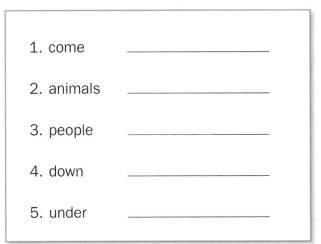

1. come   _____

2. animals   _____

3. people   _____

4. down   _____

5. under   _____

B. Read each sentence. Find the new words in the box. Write the words on the lines.

6. This word starts with **c**.

   _____ come _____

7. These 2 words name living things.

   _____   _____

8. These 2 words are location words.

   _____   _____

9. These 2 words end with **e**.

   _____   _____

10. This word has **er**.

    _____

Reading Practice

Words with Long and Short Vowels

A. Name each picture. Read the two words. Circle the word that names the picture.

1.

face / fact

2.

hi / hill

3.

be / bell

4.

wet / we

B. Now read the story. Circle the words with long e. Then circle the words with short e. Write them in the chart. Write each word one time.

(We) Like to Swim!

We like to swim. But I do not like to (get) wet! The pool is near my home. I walk there with Kim. She is my friend. We can be in the water until the bell rings. Then we have to get out. As we wait, I get dry. When they let us back in the pool, I get wet again! I like to swim so much that I do not mind if I get wet. Kim bet me I would like swimming more if I could stay dry, but I cannot do that! She is funny.

Words with long e	Words with short e
5. _____we_____	9. _____get_____
6. _____	10. _____
7. _____	11. _____
8. _____	12. _____
	13. _____
	14. _____
	15. _____

Reading Practice

Words with Long and Short Vowels

A. Name each picture. Read the two words. Circle the word that names the picture.

1.

   he / hen

2.

   he / help

3.

   hi / hit

4.

   be / bell

B. Now read the story. Circle the words with long e. Then circle the words with short e. Write them in the chart. Write each word one time.

At Home in the City

I like my home in the city. On Saturdays, Sal and I (help) at the library. (He) sits at the desk. I show the kids good books. Then I let them look around without me. At 12:00, we are done. Sometimes we stop for lunch. Then we go home. We walk down Grand Road. The city is so great! We can be home in two minutes.

Words with long e	Words with short e
5. ____he____	9. ____help____
6. _____	10. _____
7. _____	11. _____
8. _____	12. _____
	13. _____

Reading Practice

Name _____

Multisyllabic Words

A. Read each word. Write how many syllables it has.

1. pool

_____|_____

2. nickel

_____

3. moon

_____

4. garden

_____

5. basket

_____

6. napkin

_____

7. screw

_____

8. broom

_____

B. Now read the story. Circle the words with two syllables. Write each word in the chart. Then write the syllables.

(Hunting) a Pumpkin

We went to find a pumpkin at the farm. We wanted the biggest one in the field. My sister helped me look. We saw a lot of pumpkins. We also saw a snake! My mom was calling to us. The farmer told us to look in the far corner of the field. There we saw the biggest pumpkin in the whole field! Next to it was a small one. We could not carry the big pumpkin, so we picked the small one.

Word	Syllable	
9. hunting	hunt	ing
10. _____	_____	_____
11. _____	_____	_____
12. _____	_____	_____
13. _____	_____	_____
14. _____	_____	_____
15. _____	_____	_____
16. _____	_____	_____
17. _____	_____	_____
18. _____	_____	_____

Name _____

Multisyllabic Words

A. Read each word. Write how many syllables it has.

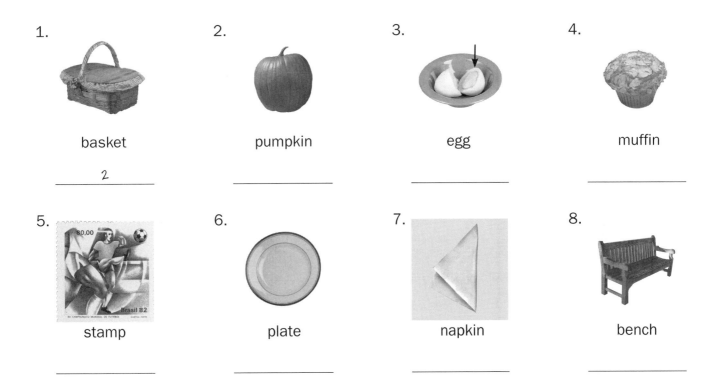

1. basket

_____2_____

2. pumpkin

_____

3. egg

_____

4. muffin

_____

5. stamp

_____

6. plate

_____

7. napkin

_____

8. bench

_____

B. Now read the story. Circle the words with two syllables. Write each word in the chart. Then write the syllables.

A (Picnic) in the Park

Jan and Chun go on a picnic. Jan packs lunch in a basket. Chun grabs a blanket. Then they put on their helmets and hop on their bikes. They ride through a tunnel, then up to Elm Road. They watch out for traffic. At the park, they see lots of children. Chun puts the blanket on the grass, and they sit down. "Let's eat," Jan says. "Do you want a sandwich?"

Word	Syllable	
9. picnic	pic	nic
10. _____	_____	_____
11. _____	_____	_____
12. _____	_____	_____
13. _____	_____	_____
14. _____	_____	_____
15. _____	_____	_____
16. _____	_____	_____

Reading Practice

Name _____

High Frequency Words, Part 1

A. Read each word. Then write it.

1. family _____

2. together _____

3. other _____

4. really _____

5. father _____

B. Read the clue. Write the word in the chart. Then write the word again in the sentence.

What to Look For	Word	Sentence
6. begins with **fam**	f a m i l y	My ___family___ loves games.
7. begins with **to**	__ __ __ __ __ __ __ __	We like to be _____ .
8. begins with **o**	__ __ __ __ __	We do _____ things, too.
9. begins with **r**	__ __ __ __ __ __	We have a _____ big family.
10. means "dad"	__ __ __ __ __ __	My _____ is an artist.

Reading Practice

High Frequency Words, Part 2

A. Read each word. Then write it.

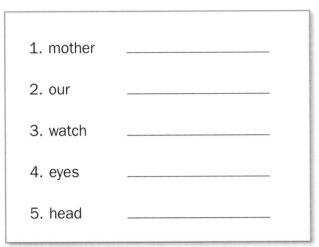

1. mother _____

2. our _____

3. watch _____

4. eyes _____

5. head _____

B. Read the clue. Write the word in the chart. Then write the word again in the sentence.

What to Look For	Word	Sentence
6. means "mom"	m o t h e r	My _____mother_____ is a writer.
7. has 3 letters	__ __ __	Friday is _____ game night.
8. ends with **tch**	__ __ __ __ __	Sometimes we _____ TV.
9. has **yes** in it	__ __ __ __	I use my _____ to do puzzles.
10. rhymes with **bed**	__ __ __ __	I think with my _____ .

Reading Practice

Name _____

Words with Long Vowels: *a_e, o_e*

A. Name each picture. Write the name.

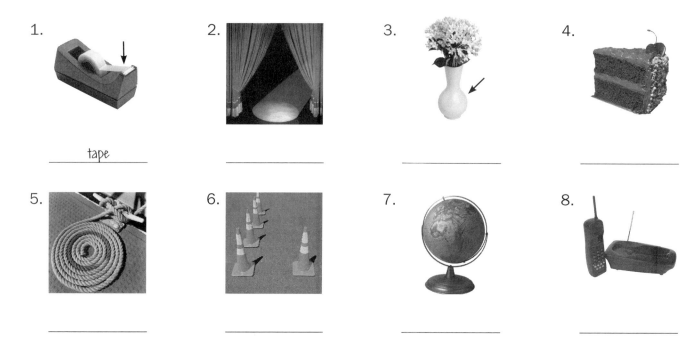

1. _____tape_____

2. _____

3. _____

4. _____

5. _____

6. _____

7. _____

8. _____

B. Now read the story. Circle the words with long *a* or long *o*. Write them in the chart. Write each word one time.

Trouble at the (Lake)

Our home is close to a lake. The lake is big. Sometimes it has big waves.

One day I take a ride and get to the lake. I gaze out. Those waves are big! I see a boy in trouble. A man comes by and spots the boy. He jumps into the water and swims out with big strokes. I shut my eyes and hope he can save the boy. And he does!

I spoke to the man. "That was very brave!" I said.

9. _____Lake_____	15. _____
10. _____	16. _____
11. _____	17. _____
12. _____	18. _____
13. _____	19. _____
14. _____	20. _____

Reading Practice

Name _____

Words with Long Vowels

A. Name each picture. Write the name.

1. _____cape_____

2. _____

3. _____

4. _____

5. _____

6. _____

7. _____

8. _____

B. Now read the story. Circle the words with long *a, i, o,* or *u*. Write them in the chart. Write each word one time.

Fun with Bill

My brother Bill (drives) a truck all around the state. When he is home, he makes life fun.

Once he put together kites for all the kids in the family. Bill had to use long, thin tubes for the frames. The wings were cloth from a torn robe. "The kites are cute," he said, "but I hope we can get them up in the air!"

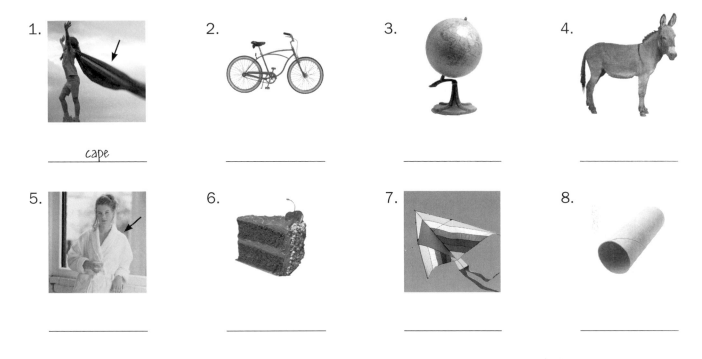

9. _____	15. _____
10. _____	16. _____
11. _____	17. _____
12. ___drives___	18. _____
13. _____	19. _____
14. _____	20. _____

Reading Practice

Words with Short and Long Vowels

A. Name each picture. Read the two words. Circle the word that names the picture.

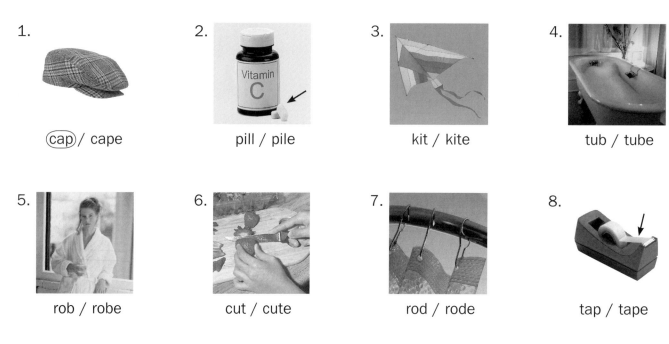

1. (cap) / cape

2. pill / pile

3. kit / kite

4. tub / tube

5. rob / robe

6. cut / cute

7. rod / rode

8. tap / tape

B. Now read the story. Circle the words with long *o* or long *i*. Underline the words with short *o* or short *i*. Write them in the chart. Write each word one time.

A Busy (Home)

We are really busy. Here <u>is</u> what a day is like. Mom drives to the pet shop. She must be there by three. The shop closes at three. Then Mom stops to get us snacks to eat. Dad helps me fix my bike, and then we scrub the stove. Pam has to watch the baby next door. At the end of the day, we like to sit down and rest. That is when we can all be together again.

9. _____Home_____	15. _____
10. _____	16. _____
11. _____	17. _____
12. _____	18. _____
13. _____	19. _____
14. _____	20. _____

Reading Practice

Name _____

Plurals

A. Name each picture. Read the two words. Circle the word that names the picture.

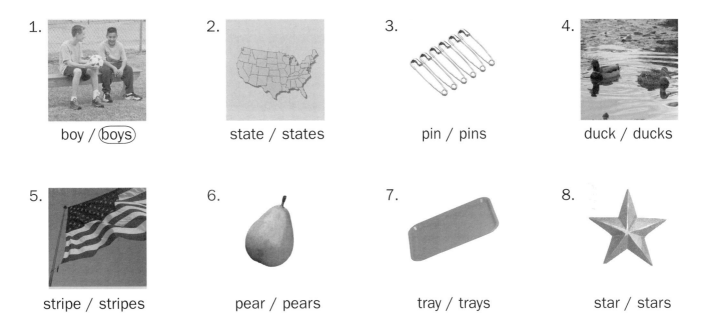

1. boy / (boys)

2. state / states

3. pin / pins

4. duck / ducks

5. stripe / stripes

6. pear / pears

7. tray / trays

8. star / stars

B. Now read the story. Circle the words that name more than one thing. Write them in the chart. Write each word one time.

(Parades) in the City

Our city has many parades for kids. The parades are a lot of fun. Girls and boys pass by in bands. They play drums and trumpets and other things. Girls do tricks with batons. We see costumes with a lot of colors. We see many pets, too. Boys and girls pass by with their dogs, cats, and snakes. Parents stand on the sidewalk and clap. They like to see the kids.

Plurals	
9. _parades_	18. _____
10. _____	19. _____
11. _____	20. _____
12. _____	21. _____
13. _____	22. _____
14. _____	23. _____
15. _____	24. _____
16. _____	25. _____
17. _____	

Name _____

High Frequency Words, Part 1

A. Read each word. Then write it.

1. places   _____

2. important   _____

3. world   _____

4. always   _____

5. or   _____

B. Find the new words. Write the words on the lines.

6. These 2 words have a **w**.

_____always_____   _____

C. Work with a partner. Follow the steps.

• Read aloud each new word in the box.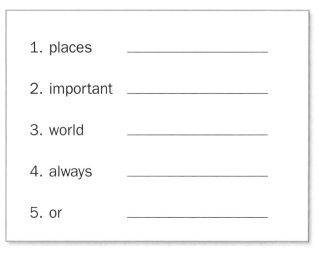

• Your partner writes the words.

• Have your partner read the words to you.

• Now you write the words on the lines below.

• Read the words to your partner.

7. _____

8. _____

9. _____

10. _____

11. _____

Name _____

High Frequency Words, Part 2

A. Read each word. Then write it.

1. river _____

2. through _____

3. once _____

4. water _____

5. below _____

B. Find the new words in the box. Write the words on the lines.

6. These 2 words have a **w**.

_____ water _____   _____

C. Work with a partner. Follow the steps.

• Read aloud each new word in the box.

• Your partner writes the words.

• Have your partner read the words to you.

• Now you write the words on the lines below.

• Read the words to your partner.

7. _____

8. _____

9. _____

10. _____

11. _____

Reading Practice

Words with Long *a*

A. Read each word. Which picture goes with the word? Write its letter.

1. tray _D_   2. stain ____   3. play ____

4. sail ____   5. midday ____   6. train ____

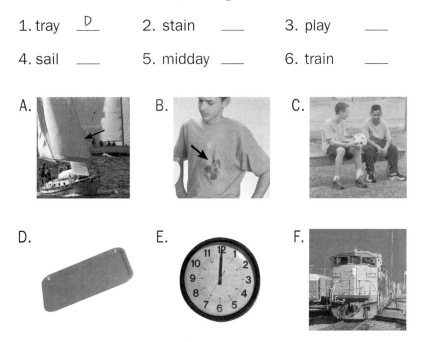

A.   B.   C.

D.   E.   F.

B. Now read the story. Circle long *a* words with *ai* and *ay*. Write them in the chart. Write each word one time.

My Grandma's Chair

My grandma has a favorite chair. She (mainly) keeps it upstairs. It has blue and purple flowers in a chain. It is big and soft. When I was little, my grandma let me play in her chair. I would pretend to be an old lady.

My grandma has gray hair, but she likes to do many things. She loves to raise the window shades early in the day. Sometimes, my grandma and I collect daisies. Then she might say, "Now, you may sit in my special chair." I always wait for her to tell me.

7. _____mainly_____	12. _____
8. _____	13. _____
9. _____	14. _____
10. _____	15. _____
11. _____	16. _____
	17. _____

Reading Practice

Words with Long *a*, Long *e*, and Long *o*

A. Read each word. Which picture goes with the word? Write its letter.

1. coast __N__   2. boat __   3. train __   4. braid __   5. road __

6. seeds __   7. paints __   8. feet __   9. sail __   10. tree __

11. tray __   12. geese __   13. crow __   14. seal __   15. tea __

A.   B.   C.   D.   E.

F.   G.   H.   I.   J.

K.   L.   M.   N.   O.

B. Name each picture below. Which words above have the same long vowel sound as the picture name? Write the words on the lines.

16. Sunday MAY 8   _train_ _____ _____ _____

17.   _____ _____ _____ _____

18.   _____ _____ _____ _____

Reading Practice

Words with Short and Long Vowels

A. Name each picture. Read the two words. Circle the word that names the picture.

1. cot / (coat)

2. tap / tail

3. bed / beach

4. sell / seal

5. pan / paint

6. pens / peas

7. cost / coast

8. rod / road

B. Now read the story. Circle the words with long *a*. Underline the words with short *a*. Write them in the chart. Write each word one time.

Mom to the Rescue!

Nick (always) goes home to see his mom once a year. He <u>packs</u> his gray bag. What if it rains? Nick gets his coat. What if it's hot? Nick gets his swim trunks. He runs to catch the train, but he forgets his bag! Mom meets Nick in Bay City. She asks, "Where is your bag?" At home, Mom looks through the house. Nick waits. Mom comes back with his old clothes!

9. ____always____	15. ____packs____
10. _____	16. _____
11. _____	17. _____
12. _____	18. _____
13. _____	19. _____
14. _____	20. _____

Multisyllabic Words

A. Read each word. Write how many syllables it has.

1. weekend

_____2_____

2. crow

_____

3. rowboat

_____

4. train

_____

5. coast

_____

6. seashell

_____

7. sunset

_____

8. stream

_____

B. Now read the story. Circle the words with two syllables. Write each word in the chart one time. Then write the syllables.

At the (Seashore)

Dean goes to the seashore on weekends. On wet days, Dean wears his raincoat down to the beach. He hunts for seashells and digs for clams. On warm days, he stays on a sailboat with his dad. They sail from sunrise to sunset. Dean loves his weekends at the seashore.

Word	Syllables	
9. seashore	sea	shore
10. _____	_____	_____
11. _____	_____	_____
12. _____	_____	_____
13. _____	_____	_____
14. _____	_____	_____
15. _____	_____	_____

Name _____

High Frequency Words, Part 1

A. Read each word. Then write it.

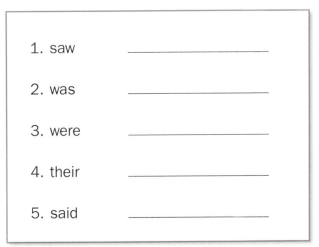

1. saw   _____

2. was   _____

3. were   _____

4. their   _____

5. said   _____

B. Write the answer to each question. Find the new words in the box. Write the words on the lines.

6. Which 2 words have 3 letters?

_____saw_____   _____

7. Which word rhymes with **her**?

_____

8. Which word has 5 letters?

_____

9. Which word rhymes with **red**?

_____

10. Which word is the past tense of **see**?

_____

Name _____

High Frequency Words, Part 2

A. Read each word. Then write it.

1. began _____

2. about _____

3. dance _____

4. thought _____

5. again _____

B. Write the answer to each question. Find the new words in the box. Write the words on the lines.

6. Which word means "started"?

_____began_____

7. Which word has 7 letters?

_____

8. Which 3 words have 2 syllables?

_____   _____   _____

9. Which 4 words have 5 letters each?

_____   _____

_____   _____

10. Which word means "once more"?

_____

Reading Practice

Verbs with -ed

A. Read each sentence. Change the word in dark type to tell about the past.

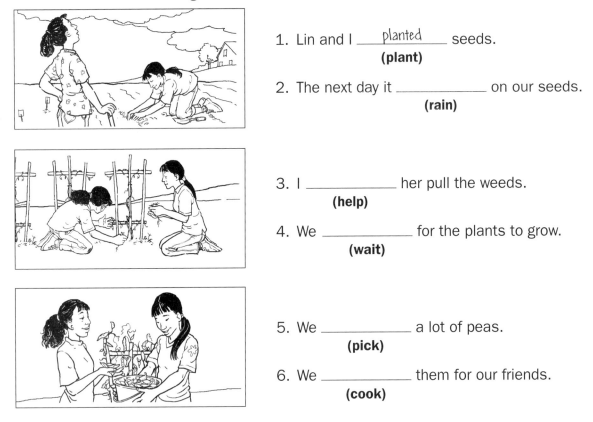

1. Lin and I ___planted___ seeds.
   (plant)

2. The next day it _____ on our seeds.
   (rain)

3. I _____ her pull the weeds.
   (help)

4. We _____ for the plants to grow.
   (wait)

5. We _____ a lot of peas.
   (pick)

6. We _____ them for our friends.
   (cook)

B. Now read the story. Circle the words with -ed. Write each word in the chart one time. Then write the root word.

We (Waited) for the Sun

On Saturday morning it rained. Kim and I waited for the sun. When it peeked through the clouds, we ran to the beach. We saw some birds and hunted for shells by the water. We cleaned the sand off the shells and put them in a box. Then we hunted for tiny crabs in the sand. Kim lifted one crab so we could see it up close.

Word with -ed	Root Word
7. ___Waited___	___wait___
8. _____	_____
9. _____	_____
10. _____	_____
11. _____	_____
12. _____	_____

Reading Practice

Verbs with -ed

A. Read each sentence. Change the word in dark type to tell about the past.

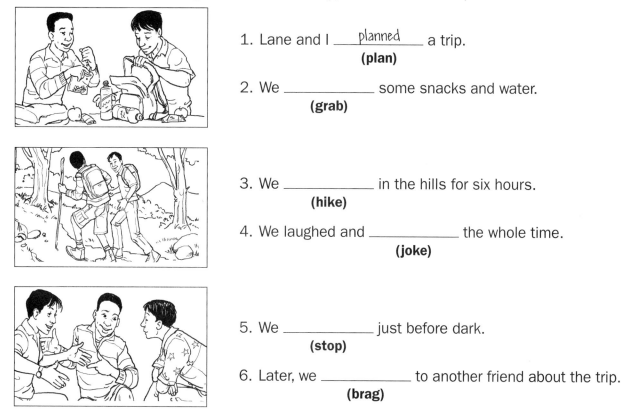

1. Lane and I ___planned___ a trip.
   (plan)

2. We _____ some snacks and water.
   (grab)

3. We _____ in the hills for six hours.
   (hike)

4. We laughed and _____ the whole time.
   (joke)

5. We _____ just before dark.
   (stop)

6. Later, we _____ to another friend about the trip.
   (brag)

B. Now read the story. Circle the words with -ed. Write each word in the chart one time. Then write the root word.

With a Friend

Ben's feet dragged as he jogged in the park. Sometimes he hated to jog by himself. He sat down on a bench to rest. Just then his friend Matt jogged by and waved.

"Matt!" Ben said. "Wait for me!" He hopped up and ran to catch up with Matt. He smiled as they ran side by side. It was more fun to jog with a friend!

Word with -ed	Root Word
7. ___dragged___	___drag___
8. _____	_____
9. _____	_____
10. _____	_____
11. _____	_____
12. _____	_____

Name _____

High Frequency Words, Part 1

A. Read each word. Then write it.

1. celebrate   _____

2. most   _____

3. young   _____

4. children   _____

5. started   _____

B. Write the answer to each question. Find the new words in the box. Write the words on the lines.

6. This word ends in **e**.

   _____ celebrate _____

7. These 2 words have **st**.

   _____   _____

8. This word is the opposite of **old**.

   _____

9. This word begins with **ch**.

   _____

10. This word is the opposite of **ended**.

   _____

Reading Practice

Name _____

High Frequency Words, Part 2

A. Read each word. Then write it.

1. beginning _____

2. change _____

3. another _____

4. only _____

5. following _____

B. Read each sentence. Find the new words in the box. Write the words on the lines.

6. These 2 words end with **ing**.

_____following_____ _____

7. This word ends with **e**.

_____

8. This word has the word **other** in it.

_____

9. Which word has 4 letters?

_____

10. This word starts with **f**.

_____

Reading Practice

Verbs with -*ing*

A. Read each sentence. Change the word in dark type to tell what is happening right now.

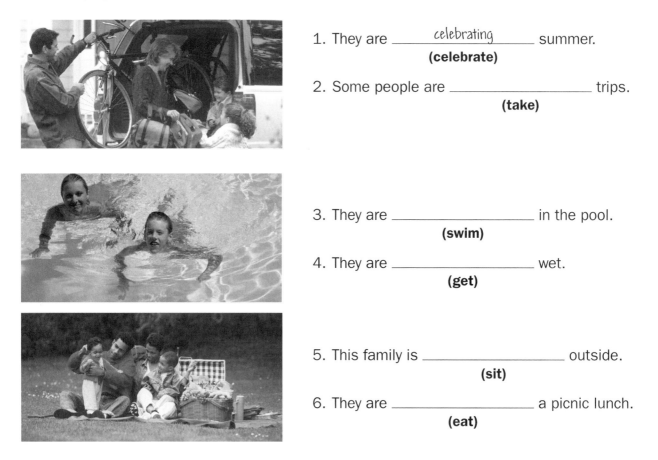

1. They are _____celebrating_____ summer.
   (celebrate)

2. Some people are _____ trips.
   (take)

3. They are _____ in the pool.
   (swim)

4. They are _____ wet.
   (get)

5. This family is _____ outside.
   (sit)

6. They are _____ a picnic lunch.
   (eat)

B. Now read the story. Circle the words with -*ing*. Write each word in the chart one time. Then write the root word.

Our School Fair

Our school fair is ⟨beginning⟩ at 2 p.m. We are taking all the games outside. Suddenly, it is raining and we are beginning to get very wet. Most of us are rushing inside. Now we are waiting for the rain to stop. Yes. The sun is shining again. The fair can begin on time.

Word with -*ing*	Root Word
7. _____beginning_____	_____begin_____
8. _____	_____
9. _____	_____
10. _____	_____
11. _____	_____
12. _____	_____

High Frequency Words, Part 1

A. Read each word. Then write it.

1. been _____

2. four _____

3. sound _____

4. caused _____

5. between _____

B. Read each sentence. Find the new words in the box. Write the words on the lines.

6. My little brother is _____four_____ years old.

7. He has always _____ fast.

8. One time, he walked away without making a _____ .

9. Kento _____ Mom a lot of worry.

10. Now he stays _____ Mom and me!

High Frequency Words, Part 2

A. Read each word. Then write it.

1. could   _____

2. almost   _____

3. life   _____

4. often   _____

5. never   _____

B. Read each sentence. Find the new words in the box. Write the words on the lines.

6. Kento _____*almost*_____ always holds Mom's hand.

7. One day Mom said he _____ walk without her.

8. Kento has been lost only once in his _____ .

9. He _____ gets lost anymore.

10. He _____ tries to stay near Mom.

Words with Long *i*

A. Name each picture. Write the name.

1. _____pie_____

2. _____

3. _____

4. _____

5. _____

B. Now read the story. Circle the words with long *i*. Write them in the chart. Write each word one time.

⟨Pie⟩ for Tonight

Li helps out in the kitchen. Today Mom is making a pie. Li washes and dries his hands. Then he rolls out Mom's dough. He puts the dough into a bright red pan. He makes it lie flat. Next Mom cuts up apples. Li mixes them with just the right amount of sugar. Mom finishes up. Then they put the pie in the oven.

The finished pie is a beautiful sight! The crust is light and flaky. The family will eat the pie tonight.

6. _____pie_____

7. _____

8. _____

9. _____

10. _____

11. _____

12. _____

13. _____

Reading Practice

Words with Long *i* or Long *u*

A. Name each picture. Write the name.

1.

    _____pie_____

2.

    _____

3.

    _____

4.

    _____

5.

    _____

6.

    _____

B. Now read the story. Circle the words with long *i* or long *u*. Write them in the chart. Write each word one time.

The (Right) Thing

Nam often helps at the senior center. He thinks it's the right thing to do. He helps in many ways. He serves pie. He brings in books and takes back the books that are (due.) In art class, Nam helps people cut and glue things. He gets the paints—bright red, yellow, blue. Four nights a year, the center has a big show. Nam wears a suit and tie. The shows are always great!

7. _____right_____	12. _____due_____
8. _____	13. _____
9. _____	14. _____
10. _____	15. _____
11. _____	

Name _____

High Frequency Words, Part 1

A. Read each word. Then write it.

1. country   _____

2. called   _____

3. lived   _____

4. house   _____

5. now   _____

B. Read each sentence. Find the new words in the box. Write the words on the lines.

6. This word means almost the same as **home**.

    _____house_____

7. This word rhymes with **cow**.

    _____

8. These words are past tense verbs.

    _____   _____

9. This word has two syllables.

    _____

10. This word is the opposite of **later**.

    _____

Name _____

High Frequency Words, Part 2

A. Read each word. Then write it.

1. American   _____

2. would   _____

3. know   _____

4. should   _____

5. also   _____

B. Read each sentence. Find the new words in the box. Write the words on the lines.

6. These two words rhyme.

_____would_____   _____should_____

7. This word has 4 syllables.

_____

8. This word has **so** in it.

_____

9. This word always begins with a capital letter.

_____

10. This word rhymes with **show**.

_____

Words with *R*-controlled Vowels

A. Name each picture. Write the name.

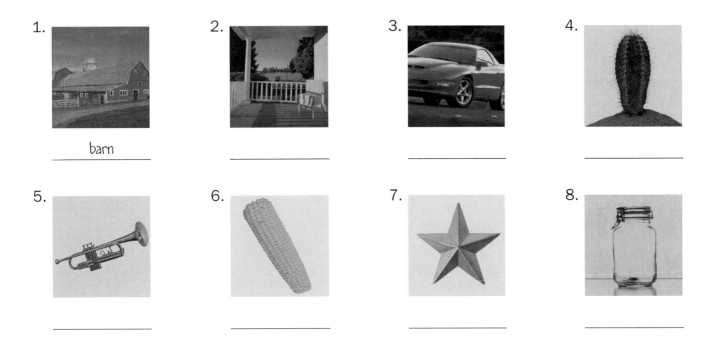

1. _____barn_____

2. _____

3. _____

4. _____

5. _____

6. _____

7. _____

8. _____

B. Now read the story. Circle the words that go in the chart.
Write them in the chart. Write each word one time.

(Storm) Watch

Carrie always enjoys watching a good storm.

She lives on a farm with a red barn and fields

of corn. When the storm blows, the rain whips

across the fields and lightning fills the sky.

Sometimes, part of the corn is torn straight

from the stalks by the wind. During one storm,

hail fell on the car and it set off the car alarm

horn.

Carrie likes a good storm far better than fair

weather. But she prefers to watch it from inside

the house!

9. _____storm_____	13. _____
10. _____	14. _____
11. _____	15. _____
12. _____	16. _____
	17. _____

Words with *R*-controlled Vowels

A. Name each picture. Write the name.

1. _____
car

2. _____

3. _____

4. _____

5. _____

6. _____

7. _____

8. _____

B. Now read the story. Circle the words that go in the chart. Write them in the chart. Write each word one time.

(Part) of a Team

Melvin is part of a rescue team. When sea birds are hurt after a storm or an oil spill, his team takes them to a yard. First they clean off the oil and dirt. Melvin holds the birds and turns them as he washes off the oil. He stays at the yard from morning until night. It is a hard job, but it is important. When the birds chirp in a happy way, Melvin is also happy. He knows that the birds may survive.

9. _____part_____
10. _____
11. _____

16. _____
17. _____
18. _____
19. _____

12. _____
13. _____
14. _____
15. _____

20. _____
21. _____
22. _____

Name _____

Words with *R*-controlled Vowels

A. Name each picture. Write the name.

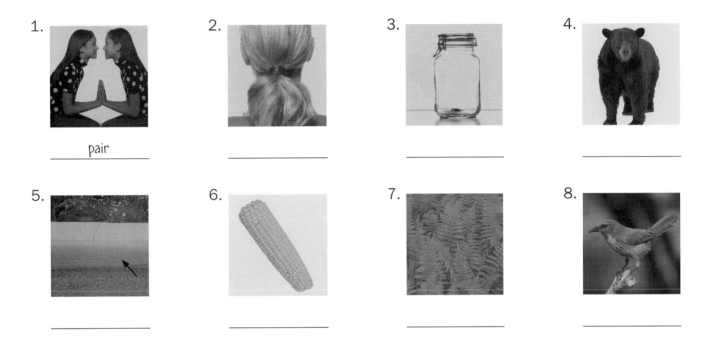

1. _____pair_____

2. _____

3. _____

4. _____

5. _____

6. _____

7. _____

8. _____

B. Now read the story. Circle the words that go in the chart.
Write them in the chart. Write each word one time.

The Race

Jill put her (hair) back in a band. She was

ready to start the race. She had worked hard.

Last time, she had come in third. This time, she

hoped to come in first.

Jill came out of the first turn in third place.

The air cooled her face. Her shirt flapped in

the wind. She felt the burn in her muscles.

She passed the last pair of runners. Jill

crossed the finish line. She was a star!

9. _____hair_____	15. _____
10. _____	16. _____
11. _____	17. _____
12. _____	18. _____
13. _____	19. _____
14. _____	

Reading Practice

Name _____

Words with *R*-controlled Vowels

A. Name each picture. Write the name.

1. _____ steer _____

2. _____

3. _____

4. _____

5. _____

6. _____

7. _____

8. _____

B. Now read the story. Circle the words that go in the chart.
Write them in the chart. Write each word one time.

A Great Guy

Lee always (cheers) people up. One year,

when I was sick, he gave me a toy deer. It was

so funny. It had a wig with long hair and a pair

of sunglasses. Last year, Lee planted tomatoes

near his house. He gave my mom a bag of big,

bright tomatoes. Lee also helps a family in

another country. He sends them socks to wear.

He brings stuffed bears to kids in Children's

Hospital.

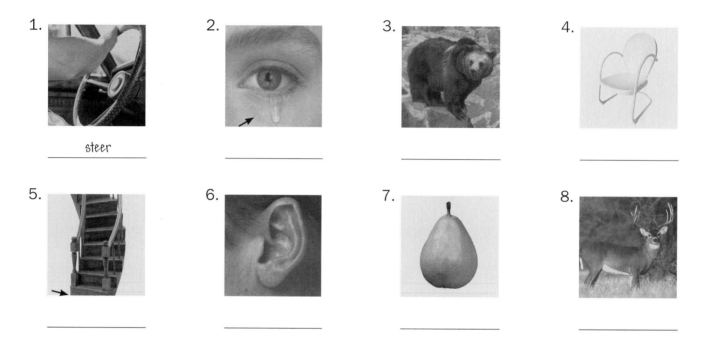

9. _____ cheers _____	13. _____
10. _____	14. _____
11. _____	15. _____
12. _____	16. _____

58

High Frequency Words, Part 1

A. Read each word. Then write it.

1. mountains _____

2. oil _____

3. found _____

4. because _____

5. few _____

B. Answer the question.

6. Which words begin with the letter **f**?

_____ found _____   _____

C. Work with a partner. Follow the steps.

- Read aloud each new word in the box.

- Your partner writes the words.

- Have your partner read the words to you.

- Now you write the words on the lines below.

- Read the words to your partner.

7. _____

8. _____

9. _____

10. _____

11. _____

Name _____

High Frequency Words, Part 2

A. Read each word. Then write it.

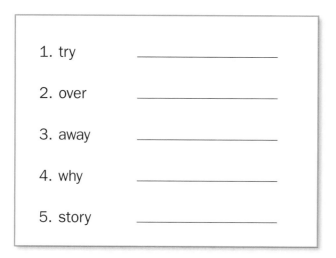

1. try _____

2. over _____

3. away _____

4. why _____

5. story _____

B. Answer the question.

6. Which words rhyme with **by**?

_____ try _____   _____

C. Work with a partner. Follow the steps.

- Read aloud each new word in the box.
- Your partner writes the words.
- Have your partner read the words to you.
- Now you write the words on the lines below.
- Read the words to your partner.

    7. _____

    8. _____

    9. _____

    10. _____

    11. _____

Reading Practice

Name _____

Types of Syllables

A. Name each picture. Read the two words. Circle the word that names the picture.

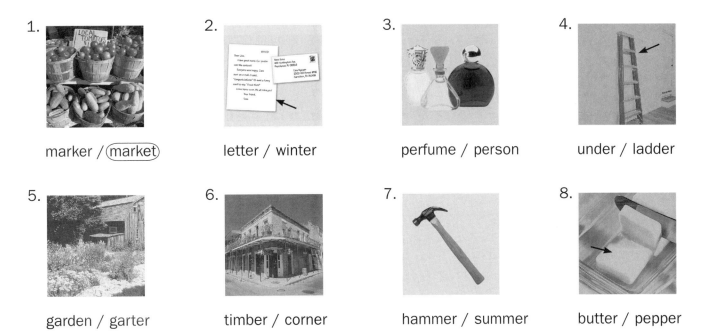

1. marker / (market)

2. letter / winter

3. perfume / person

4. under / ladder

5. garden / garter

6. timber / corner

7. hammer / summer

8. butter / pepper

B. Now read the story. Then read each word in the chart. Write the syllables in the word.

My Sister Meg

My sister Meg should live on a farm and drive a tractor. She loves to grow things! She gets perfect seeds at the market and plants them in our garden. She plants peppers for Dad and turnips for Mom. Gram asks for butter beans. Meg plants a few things for herself: plums and peas. We all help harvest what she grows. Then we cook supper. Food from the garden always tastes better!

Words	Syllables	
9. sister	sis	ter
10. perfect	_____	_____
11. garden	_____	_____
12. peppers	_____	_____
13. turnips	_____	_____
14. butter	_____	_____
15. harvest	_____	_____
16. supper	_____	_____

© NGSP & HB

61

High Frequency Words, Part 1

A. Read each word. Then write it.

1. news   _____

2. words   _____

3. much   _____

4. along   _____

5. question   _____

B. Read the clue. Write the word in the chart. Then write the word again in the sentence.

What to Look For	Word	Sentence
6. has **ew**	n e w s	I send my friend Ted my ____news____ .
7. begins with **w**	__ __ __ __ __	I write lots of _____ .
8. means "a lot"	__ __ __ __	I like him so _____ .
9. ends with **ng**	__ __ __ __ __	I went _____ to say goodbye.
10. ends with **tion**	__ __ __ __ __ __ __ __	I ask him one _____ .

Name _____

High Frequency Words, Part 2

A. Read each word. Then write it.

1. before   _____

2. miss   _____

3. example   _____

4. ever   _____

5. back   _____

B. Read the clue. Write the word in the chart. Then write the word again in the sentence.

What to Look For	Word	Sentence
6. has an **x**	e x a m p l e	Ted is an _example_ of a true friend.
7. tells when	__ __ __ __ __ __	He left _____ summer.
8. ends with **ss**	__ __ __ __	I _____ my friend.
9. has a **v**	__ __ __ __	He's the best friend I _____ had.
10. ends with **ck**	__ __ __ __	When will you come _____ ?

Name _____

Words with *y*

A. Read each word. Tell if the letter *y* is a vowel or a consonant.

1. yard

consonant

2. twenty

_____

3. sky

_____

4. happy

_____

5. year

_____

6. yarn

_____

B. Read the story. Circle the words with *y*. Write the words in the chart. Write each word one time.

(Why) I Admire Raoul Wallenburg

My class read about World War II. In one story, a man risked his life to save others. He could not be happy while other people suffered so much. He gave a lot of lucky people passports so that they could escape. He helped other people find places to hide. By the end of the war, he had helped 100,000 people.

7. Why	10. story
8. _____	11. _____
9. _____	12. _____

Name _____

Plurals: *y* + *s*, *y* to *i* + *es*

A. Read each sentence. Change the word in dark type to name more than one.

1. I have many _____hobbies_____ .
   (hobby)

2. On some _____ , I make model planes from World War II.
   (day)

3. My _____ like to help me.
   (buddy)

4. We eat lunch on _____ as we work.
   (tray)

5. We tell each other _____ about the planes.
   (story)

6. We pretend the planes are still up in the _____ .
   (sky)

B. Now read the story. Circle the plurals that end in *-ys* and *-ies*. Write each word in the chart. Then write the root word.

Dad's Favorite Hobby

My dad has many (hobbies.) The hobby he likes best is history. He likes to read about England and other countries in World War II. Sometimes he tells me stories about those days. Dad has other ways to learn about history. For example, he collects old things, like newspapers, stamps, and coins from the forties.

Word that Ends in *-ys* or *-ies*	Root Word
7. _____hobbies_____	_____hobby_____
8. _____	_____
9. _____	_____
10. _____	_____
11. _____	_____
12. _____	_____

High Frequency Words, Part 1

A. Read each word. Then write it.

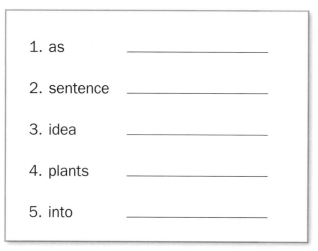

1. as   _____

2. sentence   _____

3. idea   _____

4. plants   _____

5. into   _____

B. Read each sentence. Find the new words in the box. Write the words on the lines.

6. This word is first in ABC order.

_____ as _____

7. This word starts with **s**.

_____

8. This word is something you think of.

_____

9. This word names things that grow.

_____

10. This word is the opposite of **out of**.

_____

High Frequency Words, Part 2

A. Read each word. Then write it.

1. until   _____

2. but   _____

3. seemed   _____

4. each   _____

5. made   _____

B. Read each sentence. Find the new words in the box. Write the words on the lines.

6. This word is last in ABC order.

   _____until_____

7. These two words have a **u**.

   _____   _____

8. This word starts with **s**.

   _____

9. This word has **ea**.

   _____

10. This word starts with an **m**.

   _____

Reading Practice

Words with *oi* and *oy*

A. Name each picture. Write the name.

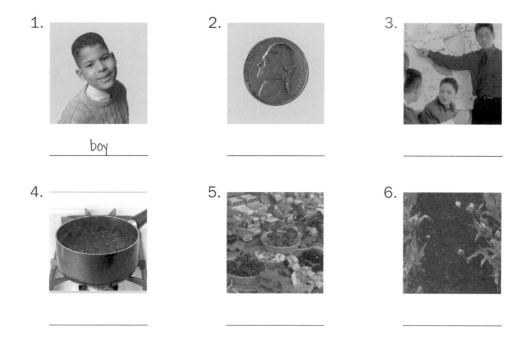

1. _____boy_____

2. _____

3. _____

4. _____

5. _____

6. _____

B. Now read the story. Circle the words with *oi* or *oy*. Write them in the chart. Write each word one time.

One (Boy's) Story

I know a boy who enjoys stories. One day he wrote his own story. It went like this.

It was a boiling hot day. A little boy went outside to plant some peppers. As he dug, he found an old toy soldier. He set the toy aside. Then he put seeds into the moist soil. When he was done, he set the toy next to the seeds. The soldier would join him in watching the seeds. They would share the joy of growing peppers.

7. _____boy_____	11. _____boiling_____
8. _____	12. _____
9. _____	13. _____
10. _____	14. _____

Name _____

Words with *oi, oy, ou,* and *ow*

A. Read each word. Which picture goes with the word? Write its letter.

1. boil _G_   2. couch ___   3. owl ___   4. crown ___   5. house ___

6. cloud ___   7. boy ___   8. crowd ___   9. coin ___   10. points ___

11. proud ___   12. soil ___   13. mouse ___   14. frown ___   15. toys ___

A.   B.   C.   D.   E.

F.   G.   H.   I.   J.

K.   L.   M.   N.   O.

B. Read each word. Find the word or words above that have the same vowel sound and spelling. Write the words on the lines.

16. join   17. joy   18. loud   19. clown

_____   _____   _____   _____

_____   _____   _____   _____

_____   _____   _____   _____

_____   _____   _____

                                   _____

Reading Practice

Words with *oo* and *ew*

A. Name each picture. Write the name.

1.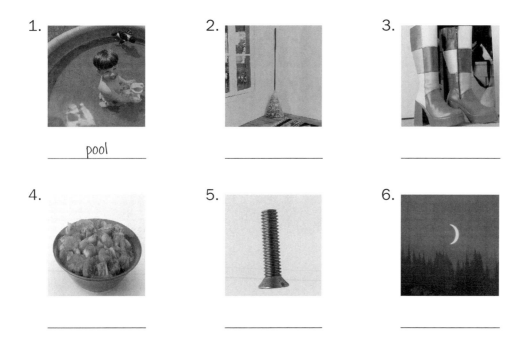
   <u>   pool   </u>

2. _____

3. _____

4. _____

5. _____

6. _____

B. Now read the story. Circle the words with *oo* or *ew*. Write them in the chart. Write each word one time.

A Winter (Stew)

What do you do on cool winter evenings? Do you watch the moon? Do you dream of summer days in the swimming pool? Do you read in your room?

I love to make a good stew. I put in a few vegetables. I add meat and broth. The stew bubbles for a while. Soon it seems ready. I scoop up a little. I taste it. It's done! The taste is always surprising and new.

7. <u> cool </u>	13. <u> stew </u>
8. _____	14. _____
9. _____	15. _____
10. _____	
11. _____	
12. _____	

Reading Practice

Words with *oo*, *ew*, *au*, *aw*, *al*, and *all*

A. Read each word. Which picture goes with the word? Write its letter.

1. mall H
2. saw ___
3. broom ___
4. salt ___
5. screw ___

6. hawk ___
7. author ___
8. moon ___
9. stew ___
10. hall ___

11. draw ___
12. boots ___
13. laundry ___
14. pool ___
15. ball ___

A.
B.
C.
D.
E.

F.
G.
H.
I.
J.

K.
L.
M.
N.
O.

B. Read each word. Find the words above that have the same sound and spelling. Write the words on the lines.

16. cool broom
_____
_____
_____

17. awful _____
_____
_____

18. small _____
_____
_____

19. chew _____
_____

20. haunted _____
_____

21. also _____

Reading Practice

High Frequency Words, Part 1

A. Read each word. Then write it.

1. friends   _____

2. asked   _____

3. walked   _____

4. trees   _____

5. air   _____

B. Answer the question.

6. Which words have **s**?

_____friends_____   _____   _____

C. Work with a partner. Follow the steps.

• Read aloud each new word in the box.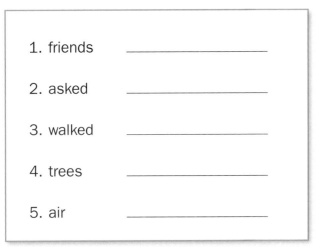

• Your partner writes the words.

• Have your partner read the words to you.

• Now you write the words on the lines below.

• Read the words to your partner.

7. _____

8. _____

9. _____

10. _____

11. _____

High Frequency Words, Part 2

A. Read each word. Then write it.

1. talked _____

2. if _____

3. even _____

4. while _____

5. such _____

B. Answer the question.

6. Which words have four letters?

_____ even _____   _____

C. Work with a partner. Follow the steps.

• Read aloud each new word in the box.

• Your partner writes the words.

• Have your partner read the words to you.

• Now you write the words on the lines below.

• Read the words to your partner.

7. _____

8. _____

9. _____

10. _____

11. _____

Reading Practice

Words with Hard and Soft c

A. Name each picture. Write the name.

1.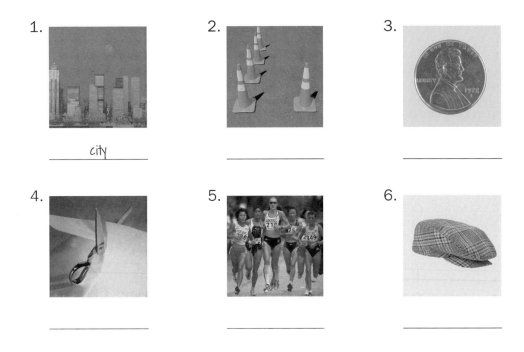

   _____city_____

2.

   _____

3.

   _____

4.

   _____

5.

   _____

6.

   _____

B. Now read the story. Circle the words with c. Write them in the chart in the correct column. Write each word one time.

Be a Winner

What (can) you do to win a race? You can work hard. Each day you can practice. Is there a safe park in your city or town? You can run there every day.

You can also take care of your body. You can eat good foods like carrots and cereal. Don't eat things like candy and cake. Drink lots of water. Aim for at least 6 cups a day.

What if you don't win the race? You still win by keeping your body in good shape.

7. _____race_____	11. _____
8. _____	12. _____
9. _____	13. _____
10. _____	14. _____
	15. _____
	16. _____

Words with Hard and Soft *c* or *g*

A. Read each word. Find the picture that goes with the word. Write its letter.

1. gum ⌐ 2. garden ___ 3. gem ___ 4. race ___

5. city ___ 6. goat ___ 7. cones ___ 8. cent ___

9. gate ___ 10. cut ___ 11. pages ___ 12. cap ___

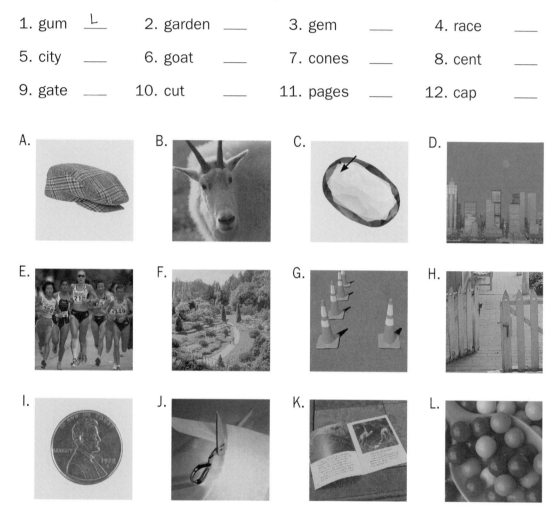

A.   B.   C.   D.

E.   F.   G.   H.

I.   J.   K.   L.

B. Name each picture below. Find the word or words in which the *c* or *g* makes the same sound. Write the words on the lines.

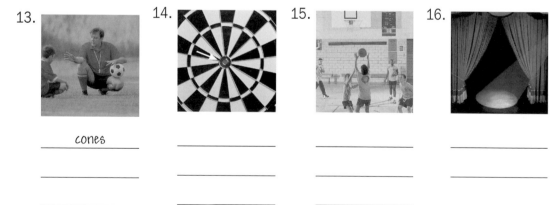

13.   14.   15.   16.

_____cones_____ _____ _____ _____

_____ _____ _____ _____

_____ _____ _____

_____

Words with Short *oo*

A. Name each picture. Write the name.

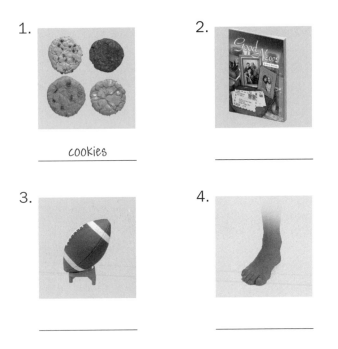

1. _____cookies_____

2. _____

3. _____

4. _____

B. Now read the story. Circle the words with *oo*. Write them in the chart.
Write each word one time.

A New (Cookie)

I baked a new kind of cookie. First I looked at

a cookbook, and then I took out what I needed.

I stood at the table, where I poured and mixed.

Finally, I put the cookies in the oven. Then I

closed the book. My brother ran in with his

football. He looked in the oven, but I shook my

head. "Not yet," I said. He sat in the eating nook

to wait. When the cookies were done, he took

a bite. "These cookies are so good," my brother

said. I love to make new things.

5. _____cookie_____	10. _____
6. _____	11. _____
7. _____	12. _____
8. _____	13. _____
9. _____	14. _____

Words with /o͝o/ or Silent Consonants

A. Name each picture. Write the name.

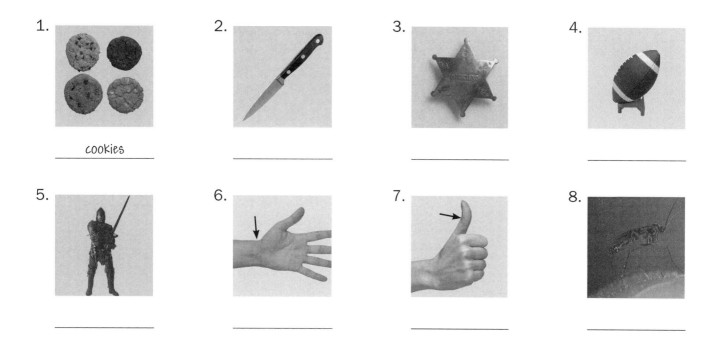

1. cookies

2. _____

3. _____

4. _____

5. _____

6. _____

7. _____

8. _____

B. Now read the story. Circle the words with /o͝o/ or silent consonants.
Write them in the chart. Write each word one time.

My Very Best

I love to play (football.) I was a good player,

but Coach said, "I know you can do better." So

one day I walked to the library to get a book

about football. I stood in the sports section a

long time and looked at many books. Finally,

I took one that had lots of tips: how to dodge

other players, throw, and even how to keep

your knees from getting wrecked. Thanks

to that book, I don't do anything wrong now.

Coach and my friends give me the thumbs up!

9. football	15. _____
10. _____	16. _____
11. _____	17. _____
12. _____	18. _____
13. _____	19. _____
14. _____	20. _____

Reading Practice

High Frequency Words, Part 1

A. Read each word. Then write it.

1. state	_____
2. than	_____
3. high	_____
4. million	_____
5. form	_____

B. Answer the questions.

6. Which words have **i**?

_____high_____   _____

7. Which words have **t**?

_____   _____

C. Read each sentence. Choose a word from the box above. Then write it in the sentence.

8. Some caves are bigger _____ others.

9. Mammoth Cave is in the _____ of Kentucky.

10. The cave is under a _____ ridge of limestone.

11. Mammoth Cave is over one _____ years old.

12. Rivers under the ground _____ lakes inside the cave.

Mammoth Cave

Reading Practice

High Frequency Words, Part 2

A. Read each word. Then write it.

1. sea	_____
2. near	_____
3. miles	_____
4. explore	_____
5. earth	_____

B. Answer the questions.

6. Which words have **ea**?

_____ *sea*   _____   _____

7. Which words start with **e**?

_____   _____

C. Read each sentence. Choose a word from the box above.
Then write it in the sentence.

8. Caves are hollow places in the _____ .

9. Caves are found inland and by the _____ .

10. Mammoth Cave is _____ the city of Bowling Green.

11. The cave is over 340 _____ long.

12. People like to _____ Mammoth Cave.

Name _____

Multisyllabic Words

A. Read each word. Write how many syllables it has.

1. crown
___1___

2. cactus
_____

3. fifty
_____

4. salt
_____

5. badge
_____

6. children
_____

7. tray
_____

8. hundred
_____

B. Now read the story. Circle the words with two syllables. Write each word in the chart. Then write the syllables in the word. Write each word one time.

The Old Days

My class went to a (hamlet) near Boston. A hamlet is a small town. We learned how children and their folks lived in the past. In the hamlet, actors dress in costumes and do things by hand. We watched a girl in a long dress churn butter. We saw a man make nails. Life was hard hundreds of years ago. When we got back to school, we had a contest to see who knew the most facts.

Word	Syllables	
9. hamlet	ham	let
10.		
11.		
12.		
13.		
14.		
15.		
16.		
17.		

Reading Practice

Name _____

Multisyllabic Words

A. Read each word. Write how many syllables it has.

1. music
   2

2. wagon
   _____

3. knife
   _____

4. stage
   _____

5. wrist
   _____

6. planet
   _____

7. city
   _____

8. asleep
   _____

B. Now read the story. Then read each word in the chart.
Write the syllables in the word.

Niagara Falls

Niagara Falls is near Buffalo, New York.
Last week, my mom and I went to visit the
falls. We stayed in a cozy cabin. We rode up the
river in a boat. The waterfalls amazed me. The
roar of the falls is so loud! The falls are about
175 feet high. They formed about 12,000 years
ago. Next time, you should come along!

Word	Syllables	
9. visit	vis	it
10. cozy	_____	_____
11. cabin	_____	_____
12. about	_____	_____
13. ago	_____	_____
14. along	_____	_____

Name _____

High Frequency Words, Part 1

A. Read each word. Then write it.

1. weigh _____

2. beautiful _____

3. special _____

4. own _____

5. any _____

B. Read the clue. Write the word in the chart. Then write the word again in the sentence.

What to Look For	Word	Sentence
6. rhymes with **say**	w e i g h	Pumpkins can ___weigh___ 20 pounds.
7. ends with **ful**	_ _ _ _ _ _ _ _ _	My berries are _____ .
8. starts with **sp**	_ _ _ _ _ _ _	Fall is a _____ time.
9. means "belongs to me"	_ _ _	I want my _____ garden.
10. rhymes with **many**	_ _ _	There isn't _____ sun.

Reading Practice

Name _____

High Frequency Words, Part 2

A. Read each word. Then write it.

1. indoors _____

2. warm _____

3. healthy _____

4. cold _____

5. outdoors _____

B. Read the clue. Write the word in the chart. Then write the word again in the sentence.

What to Look For	Word	Sentence
6. means "inside"	i n d o o r s	I stay _indoors_ and read.
7. is the opposite of **cool**	__ __ __ __	Plants grow in the _____ sun.
8. means "not sick"	__ __ __ __ __ __ __	The pumpkins are _____ .
9. is the opposite of **hot**	__ __ __ __	Today is windy and _____ .
10. means "outside"	__ __ __ __ __ __ __ __	I work _____ under the sky.

Reading Practice

Suffixes: *-ly, -y*

A. The suffix *-ly* changes an adjective to an adverb. The suffix *-y* changes a noun to an adjective. Read each sentence. Add *-ly* or *-y* to the word in dark type to complete the sentence.

1.

The sun is **bright**. It shines
___brightly___ .

2.

The drums are **loud**. The boy plays _____ .

3.

This room is a **mess**. It is _____ .

4.

The machine digs up **dirt**. It gets _____ .

5.

He is a **safe** rider. He rides _____ .

6.

The boy plays in the **sand**. He gets _____ .

B. Now read the story. Circle each word with the suffix *-ly* or *-y*. Write the words in the chart. Then write the root words.

In the Garden

Kim's alarm clock rang (loudly) She still felt sleepy! She dressed quickly in old pants and tiptoed softly into the garden. It was a warm, windy day. Kim bent down and dug in the rocky soil. Suddenly her hand hit something. She dug a little more and discovered a big, brown potato. Kim pulled it out of the dirt. "It must weigh five pounds," she thought. "It could make a healthy meal for six people."

Word with *-ly*	Root Word
7. ___loudly___	___loud___
8. _____	_____
9. _____	_____
10. _____	_____

Word with *-y*	Root Word
11. _____	_____
12. _____	_____
13. _____	_____
14. _____	_____

Reading Practice

Suffixes: *-ful, -less*

A. The suffix *-ful* means "full of." The suffix *-less* means "without." Add *-ful* or *-less* to each word to make a new word. Write the word that goes with each picture.

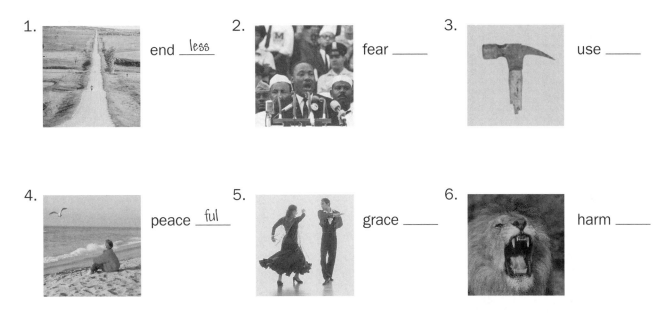

1. end <u>less</u>

2. fear _____

3. use _____

4. peace <u>ful</u>

5. grace _____

6. harm _____

B. Now read the story. Circle each word with the suffix *-ful* or *-less*. Write the words in the chart. Then write the root words.

Sun and Wind

Mike looked at his grape vines. The hot sun beat down on the plants. A warm wind began to blow. Mike was worried because wind can be (harmful) to grapes. The wind blew for days. It seemed endless. "I hope my vines survive," Mike thought. "I wish I could do something, but I am helpless." He felt so useless. At last, the wind stopped. It was peaceful again. The grape vines still looked healthy. Mike felt very thankful.

Word with *-ful*	Root Word
7. harmful	harm
8. _____	_____
9. _____	_____

Word with *-less*	Root Word
10. _____	_____
11. _____	_____
12. _____	_____

Reading Practice

Prefixes: *re-, un-*

A. The prefix *re-* can mean "again." The prefix *un-* can mean "not" or "the opposite of." Add *re-* or *un-* to each word to make a new word. Write the word that goes with the picture.

1. _re_ build

2. _____ write

3. _____ place

4. _____ lock

5. _____ happy

6. _____ cut

B. Now read the story. Circle each word with the prefix *re-* or *un-*. Write the words in the chart. Then write the root words.

Miller's Farm

At Miller's Farm you can (relive) the past. You can taste fresh, unsalted peanuts. You can also make your own peanut butter. First, untie a big sack and take some peanuts. Be sure to retie the sack. Take off the shells. Then, put the peanuts in a grinder. Grind the peanuts to make peanut butter. Uncover a jar and fill it. Put the cover on the jar. Refill the grinder to make more peanut butter.

Word with *re-*	Root Word
7. _____relive_____	_____live_____
8. _____	_____
9. _____	_____

Word with *un-*	Root Word
10. _____	_____
11. _____	_____
12. _____	_____

Name _____

High Frequency Words, Part 1

A. Read each word. Then write it.

1. show	_____
2. right	_____
3. close	_____

B. Read each question. Find the new words in the box. Write the words on the lines.

4. Which words name actions?

_____ show _____   _____

5. Which word is the opposite of "left"?

_____

6. Which word can be both a verb and a noun?

_____

7. Which word can mean "near"?

_____

8. Which words can be adjectives?

_____   _____

Name _____

High Frequency Words, Part 2

A. Read each word. Then write it.

1. watch	_____
2. kind	_____

B. Read each question. Find the new words in the box. Write the words on the lines.

3. Which word names an action?

_____watch_____

4. Which word is an adjective?

_____

5. Which word can be both a verb and a noun?

_____

6. Which word means "look at"?

_____

7. Which word means "type of"?

_____

Name _____

Types of Syllables

A. Name each picture. Read the two words. Circle the word that names the picture.

1.

middle / (pickle)

2.

table / little

3.

circle / gentle

4.

beetle / eagle

5.

apple / able

6.

candle / huddle

7.

twinkle / title

8.

turtle / purple

B. Now read the story. Circle the words with a consonant + *-le*. Write them in the chart.

A Native American (Fable)

Native Americans tell stories about Coyote. In one story, Coyote sees a little star that twinkles like a candle. "Come close!" Coyote yells. "I want to dance with you." The star floats down and he grabs it. He soars like an eagle, high over Table Rock. He isn't able to hang on. His hands slip and he tumbles down. Splat! He lands by a beetle. What did Coyote learn? It's simple: You can't do everything you want.

Long Vowel in First Syllable	Short Vowel in First Syllable
9. _____Fable_____	14. _____little_____
10. _____	15. _____
11. _____	16. _____
12. _____	17. _____
13. _____	18. _____

Reading Practice

Types of Syllables

A. Name each picture. Read the two words. Circle the word that names the picture.

1.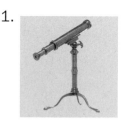
(telescope) / tolerate

2.
fourteen / fifteen

3.
reptile / record

4.
aboard / alone

5.
beneath / between

6.
remain / repeat

7.
fearful / faithful

8.
celebrate / calculate

B. Now read the story. Circle the two-syllable words. Find the vowel pattern. Write each word in the chart. Write each word one time.

Apollo (Thirteen)

In 1970, a space capsule tried to reach the moon. However, a mistake caused two air tanks to explode. No one knew the reason for the mistake. Yet the craft could not go to the moon. The astronauts had to survive, so they released the tanks. Teams on Earth watched and helped the crew succeed. They exclaimed joyfully when the astronauts got home alive.

Two Vowels Work Together	Vowel and *e* Work Together
9. _____Thirteen_____	14. _____capsule_____
10. _____	15. _____
11. _____	16. _____
12. _____	17. _____
13. _____	18. _____

Reading Practice

Name _____

Multisyllabic Words

A. Read each word. Write how many syllables it has.

1. eagle

____2____

2. unbuckle

_____

3. faithful

_____

4. superstar

_____

5. telescope

_____

6. replace

_____

7. candle

_____

8. unafraid

_____

B. Now read the story. Circle the words with more than one syllable. Write each word in the chart one time. Then write the syllables in the word.

The (Republic) of Blues

My band is called The Republic of Blues. A lot of faithful fans come to our shows. They love our kind of music. I play the steel drums and Clive sings. He likes to rearrange old songs, too. I like his simple love songs best. I hope he does not leave the band. I would be so unhappy. I don't think I could replace him. I hope we will both be stars one day!

Word	Syllables		
9. _Republic_	_Re_	_pub_	_lic_
10. _____	____	____	
11. _____	____	____	
12. _____	____	____	____
13. _____	____	____	
14. _____	____	____	____
15. _____	____	____	

Decodable Passage 1

A Lap, a Cat Nap, and a Pal

Pam stands at the window and claps.

"Dad! Dad! I can see a van, and I can see a man in a tan cap. The man has a fat cat. Can I go and gab, Dad?" Pam asks.

Dad hangs up a damp rag and says, "Okay, Pam. I can go, too."

Pam ran fast to the van. Pam says, "Hi. I am Pam. I saw your van and your cat."

"I am Frank," says the man in the tan cap. "And my cat is Max. This is our brand new home." Dad and Frank shake hands.

"Can I pat Max?" asks Pam.

"You can pat Max," Frank says. "Max is a fan of pats, and Max is a fan of laps, too."

Pam had a plan.

Pam sat down, and Max sat on her lap. Max had a cat nap on Pam! Max is a fan of laps and naps! Pam, Frank, Dad, and Max are pals. Pam is glad.

Words with short a

and	claps	Frank	has	naps	rag
asks	Dad	gab	lap	pal	ran
at	damp	glad	laps	pals	sat
brand	fan	had	man	Pam	stands
can	fast	hands	Max	pat	tan
cap	fat	hangs	nap	plan	van
cat					

High Frequency Words

go	home	new

Decodable Passage 2

Jan Has Hot Dogs!

Dad, Mom, Tad, Sal, Tom and Rob sit at a hot dog hut. Jan, a gal in a cap, gets a menu for Dad. Then, Jan gets one for Mom, Tad, Tom, Sal, and Rob. Dad, Mom, Tad, Tom, Sal, and Rob read. Next, Jan runs and gets a fat pad. "Hot dogs?" Jan asks.

"Hot dog!" answers Dad.

"Hot dog!" answers Mom.

"Hot dog!" answers Tad.

"Hot dog!" answers Sal.

"No hot dog," Tom answers.

"No hot dog?" Mom asks Tom.

"No hot dog?" Dad asks Tom.

"No hot dog!" answers Tom. "A can of ham, fat yams, hot cod, toast and jam. Jam on top—not a pat, not a dab—a gob!"

That leaves Rob. Rob sits up. "Hot dog!" says Rob. "A fat, fat hot dog!"

Jan gets hot dogs for Dad, Mom, Sal, and Tad. Jan gets a big, fat hot dog for Rob. And for Tom, Jan gets a can of ham, hot cod, a fat yam, and toast with a gob of jam on top.

Words with short o

cod	gob	Mom	on	Tom
dog	hot	not	Rob	top

High Frequency Words

next	one	then

Decodable Passage 3

A Dog and a Cat at Last

Tom and Pam are pals. Pam has a fat cat, Max, and Tom has a dog, Bob. "A cat is a blast," says Pam. "But I wish I had a dog *and* a cat! A dog can jog and romp with you. A cat can not jog or romp." Tom is glad he has a dog and not a cat. Tom is not fond of cats at all.

Soon, Bob the dog has puppies. Bob is a gal, not a guy, and now Bob is a mom. Tom brings Pam a small, tan dog in a box. Pam is glad to see Tom.

Max is glad, too. Max hops on Tom's lap. "Scat, Max!" says Tom, but Max is a brat. Max likes the spot on Tom's lap and will not scat. Max flops flat and has a nap.

"You can pat Max," says Pam. "Max will not snap at you." Tom pats Max.

"You can pat the dog, Pam," says Tom, and Pam pats her brand new dog, Spot.

Spot pants fast and wags a lot. "Spot likes me!" claps Pam. "I am very glad."

Tom nods. "I am glad, too," says Tom.

Pam is glad. She has a fat cat and a dog—at last.

Words with short *a*, short *o*

a	brat	flat	hops	nap	romp
am	can	flops	jog	nods	scat
and	cat	fond	lap	not	snap
at	claps	gal	last	on	Spot
blast	dog	glad	lot	Pam	tan
Bob	fast	has	Max	pants	Tom
box	fat	had	mom	pats	wags
brand					

High Frequency Words

new

Decodable Passage 4

Dip Tips

Tim has six tips on how to fix hot dip:

1. First grab a pad. Jot down what you will need. Is it a lot? Did you jot ham, a can of yams, jam, cod, hot dogs, or a bag of figs? Dill is tasty with hot dip. Add dill to the pad.
2. Fix the dip. Ham can have a lot of fat on it. Fat is bad. Lop it off. Do not miss a bit. Big figs can have pits. Get rid of the fig pits. Cod can have fins. Rip off the fins. Add a bit of dill.
3. Next mix the dip in a big pot or in a large pan. Do not mix it in a box. Do not mix it in a can. Do not fill it to the top.
4. Fit a lid on the pot. It can be a glass lid or it can be a tin lid.
5. Mix the dip six times: mix, mix, mix, mix, mix, mix. Do not sit. Do not miss a mix! It is a big, hot job.
6. Then sit. Try a bit of dip. Do not eat a lot.

Using Tim's six tips, your dip can not miss! His dip is tops!

Words with short _i_

big	fig	his	mix	rip	Tim's
bit	figs	is	pig	sit	tips
dill	fins	it	pits	six	will
dip	fix	miss	rid	Tim	

High Frequency Words

First	Then	Next	large

Decodable Passage 5

Jim and Big Gus

Jim is in a bad, bad rut. He wants to fix a hot meal for his pal, Big Gus. He wants to mix up something fun to eat at six. But, what will it be? Jim has to think fast.

Can he fix a pan of hot ham? Jim bit his lip. A pan of hot ham is not bad, but it is not great. "Hot ham is a bit of a risk," Jim thinks.

Will Gus like clam dip? No. Clam dip will be a dud!

Jim thinks. Will Gus like crab crisp? No. Crab crisp is not a fun meal.

Will Gus eat a vat of ox stew? No. Ox stew is a bit bland.

Just then, Jim has an idea. Jim grabs a pot and drops a big pat of butter and an egg into it. Jim drops in a cup of flour and a bit of mint. And then, Jim drops in something secret! Finally, Jim puts a lid on the pot and sits.

At six, there is a rap, rap, rap on the door. It is Big Gus.

"It is six, and here I am!" says Big Gus.

"Sit, Gus!" says Jim. "I will grab the pot."

Big Gus had a small bit of the food.

"What is in it?" Big Gus asks.

"Fig!" answers Jim.

"Fig?" asks Big Gus.

"Fig," says Jim. "It is fig pudding."

"Mmm," says Big Gus.

"Is it good and fun?" asks Jim.

"It is!" answers Big Gus.

Words with short *u*

but	dud	Gus	rut	up
cup	fun	nut	sun	

High Frequency Words

eat	small	something	then	there

Decodable Passage 6

Dig into a Bun!

Tim put a mat on the table for Bud. Then Tim got Nan a mat and one for himself. Tim put a small plate on each mat. Tim put a large mug on each mat. Then Tim got a big jug of milk.

"Sit!" said Tim. "Go on! Sit! Sit! Sit!" Bud sat and Nan sat, but Tim did not sit. Tim said, "I will sit, but I must get something first. "What is it?" ask Bud and Nan. "Is it a gift for us?"

Tim got a big, flat pan. "It is not a gift, but you will like it. It is six plum buns in a pan! I made six plum buns for us!"

"Do not drop the pan, Tim!" said Nan. "Do not slip or trip, Tim!" said Bud. Tim did not trip or slip, and he did not drop the plum buns. Tim sat and took a big, fat, hot bun. "Have one," said Tim. "Dig in! Eat up!" Bud took a big, fat, hot bun.

Bud has a sip and lifts a bun to his lips. "Mmm," said Bud. "A hot bun is not bad with milk! I will dunk my bun in milk, and I will try to not drip it on the rug!"

"Grab a bun, Nan!" said Bud. "Grab a big, fat, hot bun, and dunk it in milk!

"I will!" said Nan. And that is just what she did! What fun!

Words with short *i*, short *u*

big	drip	his	just	plum	Tim
Bud	dunk	hot	lifts	rug	trip
buns	flat	in	lip	sip	us
but	fun	is	milk	sit	will
did	gift	it	mug	slip	
dig	grab	jug	must	six	

High Frequency Words

eat	go	one	something
first	large	small	then

Decodable Passage 7

Chad Can Chop

Mom asks, "Chad, I know it is dull, but will you help make lunch?"

Chad says, "You bet I will! I can cut a big bunch of carrots. I can chop nuts for a batch of cookies. I can mix a jug of red punch. It is not dull. It will be fun!" Chad is such a good kid.

Mom tells Chad, "Fetch a bunch of carrots, a bag of chips, and the red punch mix." Chad did.

"Can I eat a chip?" Chad asks. Mom nods. Chad munches. Munch, munch, munch!

Chad got a bit of chip on his chin.

"You can mix the punch, Chad," says his mom. "Add a pinch of sugar to the punch. I will fix us a big batch of cookies. We can munch on them at lunch. Sit on the bench. We can chat."

Chad sat. Mom got a cup of chips. Mom got a cup of nuts. Buzz— hot cookies! Chad sets the cookies up on the sill to chill." Mom gets napkins. Chad digs in.

"Yum, yum, yum!" Chad says. The cookies are not rich, but Chad has his fill. Chad hugs his mom.

Words with _ch, tch_

batch	Chad	chin	chop	munches	punch
bench	chat	chip	lunch	pinch	rich
bunch	chill	chips	munch		

High Frequency Words

| eat | make | says |

Decodable Passage 8

Hens on Eggs

Eggs sell like pop in July—fast. As it is the job of a hen to sit on eggs, we hens get fed well. At six, when the sun is up, we get let out of our pen to fill up on bugs. I love to catch wet, rich gobs of bugs! At ten, when the sun is hot, we get fed corn in a big box. (Yes, it is less tasty than bugs.) At six at night, when the sun sets, we get fed corn in our pen.

Life as a hen is fun, yet it is a bit hard at times. Let me tell you about Meg. Meg is not a pet dog or a cat. Meg is not a pig. Meg is not the vet. Meg is a red fox! A fox and a hen are not pals!

On Sunday, the latch in our pen fell open. A cat yell got me up from bed, and I met Meg in the pen. Well, you can bet I let out a yell. But, Meg and I had a chat. Meg had a den that was such a big, wet mess. The hen pen was not a mess. Hens are not pigs! Meg did not need eggs. Meg did need a bed. I let Meg nap until six, but I did not let her get one egg!

Well, Meg and I became pals, but I can tell you, it is not all bugs, naps, and fun as a hen. A hen has a job—it is to sit on eggs.

Words with short *e*

bet	get	Meg	pet	tell	wet
den	hen	mess	red	ten	yell
eggs	hens	met	sell	vet	yes
fed	let	pen	sets	well	yet
fell					

High Frequency Words

from	love	one	open	when

Decodable Passage 9

Get Set, Run

Ted pats his dog, Jem. There is a big web with bugs on it and a lot of wet logs, but no sun. Ten minutes pass. The rain has not let up yet, but Ted and his dog set off for home.

Ted's wet hat and wet bag sag. The path is wet, too; it is much like a mud pit. "Do not sit in the mud, Jem!" Ted tells Jem, but Jem sits and gets wet. She is a big wet mess. "Stop it, Jem!" yells Ted. Jem rubs mud on Ted. Ted has gobs of mud on him. It will be a big job to get the mud off his legs.

Suddenly, his hair stands up in the chill air. Jem sits up, too. Ted and Jem can hear a hiss on the hill. I bet it is a fox cub! "Jem," Ted begs, "we must get out of here. Get set, run!"

Jem runs and runs. "Jem!" yells Ted. "Get Mom!" Ted runs as fast as his legs can go, but his bag pops open. His bug net is in the bag. "Yes," thinks Ted. "I can catch it with this." Ted runs behind a big tree and gets the net set. Something runs by, and Ted runs at it with his net.

It is a chipmunk, and Ted did not catch it! "I am such a silly kid!" says Ted. "Well, I am glad Jem can not see my red face."

Words with short *e*

begs	hems	mess	Ted	well	yet
bet	Jem	net	tells	wet	
get	legs	red	ten	yell	
gets	let	set	web	yes	

High Frequency Words

face	go	home	open	something	there

Decodable Passage 10

Bad Luck

Chuck has bad luck. When he was a baby, Chuck sat on a duck. The duck got very mad and bit him. As a little boy, Chuck fell in a large, wet patch of mud and muck. He had as much mud and muck on him as a rock, so a duck sat in his lap and, when Chuck let out a yell, the duck bit him. As a kid, Chuck pet a pup on the back, and something made the pup run. The pup ran by a duck and scared it. Yes, the duck got mad and bit Chuck.

Jack has bad luck as well. As a baby, Jack pet a cat on the neck, and the cat got mad and bit Jack. As a tot, Jack put his socks in the sun, and the socks got hot. A cat had a nap on those hot socks, and when Jack tried to get his socks back, the cat bit him. As a kid, Jack had a big red sack. A cat got in it, and yes, it bit Jack as Jack tried to pick it up.

Well, get this—now Chuck is a vet, and Jack is a vet, too! A vet has to help sick pups, cats, hens, chicks, ducks, and pigs. If a hen pecks a vet, the vet has to help. If a pig kicks a vet, the vet has to help. You can bet Chuck will get bit by ducks and Jack will get bit by cats. There are no ifs, ands, or buts about it—Chuck and Jack have bad, bad luck!

Words with *ck*

back	duck	luck	neck	rock	sick
Chuck	Jack	muck	pick	sack	socks

High Frequency Words

large	something	there	when

Decodable Passage 11

A Fish Wish

Our ship sits in fog. I am sad, for I can not see any fish in fog, and it is my wish to catch a big fish.

As I wish for sun in the chill, dim hush, Dad yells. "Tish! Get a mop. We can't fish, but we can mop decks. We can dab muck in gaps to fix the hull. "I wish I did not have to dash to get a mop and a tub of muck, which I'll use to fill holes in the hull. But, the sun is not up yet, so I get a mop and a tub of muck.

Dad asks, "Can you fix a mesh net? It has a big gash in it." I pick up the net and rush to find a sewing kit. I wish I did not have to patch a net. Fog has us shut in and we can not fish, so I patch the gash in the mesh.

I am in shock. The sun has gotten rid of the fog! I fetch a pole and net. Will I get my wish and catch a big fish? I shut my eyes and wish for a bit of luck.

We pass wet rocks. Ducks dip, gulls chat, and shells catch the sun. A fin pops up. It is a fish.

"Dad!" I yell. "It is a big fish!" I tug. The fish tugs back, but I win. With a tap, a large cod hits the deck. It fills a net and rips the mesh. But I am not mad. I got my wish to catch a fish.

Words with *sh*

dash	gash	mesh	shells	shock	Tish
fish	hush	rush	ship	shut	wish

High Frequency Words

find	large	use

Decodable Passage 12

Seth at Six

Seth ran up the path. Seth rang the bell. His mom and dad had told him to meet them at this house at six. Seth had to dash to get there at six. It was six on the dot when he rang the bell. Seth rang the bell again—RING, RING—but did not hear a thing. Then he sat on a bench in a patch of hot sun with his back to the door. A fat cat jumped up and sat on his lap. Seth sang a song as he sat in the hot sun with that cat.

Then a thin, fit man with a tan dog ran from a red house. This man sang a song as he ran, but it was a different song than Seth had sung. When the thin man and the tan dog ran by, the fat cat hid from the dog behind a shed.

Seth had turned back to catch the cat when he heard a thud, then a BONG, then a BAM, BONG, BONG! The thin man had whacked a trash can with a big lid as he ran. The lid went BING, BONG, BONG when it hit the ground. Then the man fell on the lid. Seth got up to help the thin man.

When the cat came back, Seth sat in the sun with the cat on his lap. It was now ten past six. Seth wished his mom and dad would show up.

Words with _th_

path	than	them	thin	this	with
Seth	that	then	thing	thud	

Words with _wh_

whacked	when

Words with _ng_

bang	bong	ring	song	thing

High Frequency Words

different	from	then	there	when

Decodable Passage 13

My Next Trip

When I plan my next trip, I will pack a trunk and hope it will be grand. Where will I end up? I do not yet know.

Will I cross the sea in a blimp? Will I hop on a tram? Will I go two or three miles? Will I go 200? And, will I land where colts run in the tall grass? Where I can stroll on the sand and catch a crab in a trap for lunch? Where I can splash in a pond? I do not yet know.

Will I stop for 10 days? Will I stop for 20? Will I find enough different things to snack on? Will I drink milk in a glass? Will I flop onto beds of brass and silk? Will I rest on mats in the dust? Will my trip be bliss or just bland? I do not yet know.

When I get back, will I be sad? Will I brag to my pals? Will I hug my dog and cat and be glad to plop onto a soft bed that I know?

Until I go on my next trip, I will not know if it will stink or if it will be the best. But I will tell you when I get back. In fact, the first thing I will do when I go on my next trip is this: I will grab a stamp and send you a letter.

Words with initial and final blends

best	cross	glad	milk	silk	stop
bland	drink	glass	plan	snack	stroll
blimp	drop	grab	plop	soft	tram
brag	dust	grand	pond	splash	trap
brass	end	grass	rest	stamp	trip
colts	flop	land	sand	stink	trunk

High Frequency Words

different	enough	final	three	two	when

Decodable Passage 14

The Quest for Gold

Gold! One reason that men try to find brand new land is that they hope to find gold. When bold men try to find an old city with a lot of gold, they hope that they will be rich. The quest for gold and land can make even a kind man go wild. The quest for gold and land can give even a kind man a cold, cold heart.

An old book from the past tells of a rich king who has a lust for gold. He would grind his gold until it became dust. He would mix the gold dust with mud and rub the wet stuff on his skin. Then, he would bolt into a big, cold pond. All the people thought that he had lost his mind!

That tale of the gold king became a tale about a golden city with thick gold walls. A long brick path winds through this golden city. In the city, an adult or a child can stroll past golden homes, hop on top of golden posts, and ride in rigs down long golden streets.

You cannot tell men on a quest for gold that golden cities do not exist and never have. In the past, those men did not see that they could go to the end of the map, but they would not find a land of gold. So, the king, his pond, and the golden city can only be found in books and in rich minds.

Words with word patterns and multisyllabic words

be	child	go	he	old	the
became	cold	gold	kind	posts	wild
bold	even	golden	mind	so	winds
bolt	find	grind	minds	stroll	

High Frequency Words

all	find	home	new	then
city	from	long	one	use
down	go	make	people	when

Decodable Passage 15

Jane Doesn't Help!

Jane's father told her that she had to help him clean out the attic tomorrow. Jane had other plans, so she was not happy. As Jane came up the steps, she saw a crib, a bed, games, pots and pans, a hose, skates, and picture frames. Then she saw a lampshade, a desk, a rake, a box of old plates, a cane, fake plants, a fake snake, and a globe. Her father said, "If we work together, we can get rid of this junk in no time!"

Jane looked around. "That's the pole I had to catch my first fish. Those are my first skates. And, this is the bat I had to hit a home run. I made this puppet in second grade! This stuff is not junk! What's in this box, Dad?" asked Jane.

"Family pictures," said Dad. This is Grandma Rose as a baby. And, this is Grandpa Gabe when he was ten."

"Save them!" yelled Jane.

"Look at these, Jane. Grandma brought these plates and cups from Finland when she came here on a ship. Grandma's wedding dress is in this big box."

"Save those things! I will take them!" said Jane as she looked around. "I can put this crate next to my bed and set a vase on it. And, save this globe, this lamp, this game, this rug, this puppet, this shell, this jump rope, this red cape, and this whole case of plastic cups."

"You are not helping a bit, Jane!" laughed Dad. "I'll just do this job alone."

Words with long *a*

came	crate	game	Jane's	rake	snake
cane	fake	games	made	save	take
cape	frames	Jane	plates	skates	vase
case	Gabe				

Words with long *o*

alone	home	pole	Rose	whole
globe	hose	rope	those	

High Frequency Words

family	from	home	other	second	together
father	her	next	out	then	when
first					

Decodable Passage 16

Five Things a Fine Home Has

Most fine homes include many fine things. Some are things that people just like to have. Others are things they *must* have. Here are five things a home must include.

A fine home has a stove. A stove is used to make healthful food, on which a family likes to dine. A stove can be used to bake cupcakes, make an egg for lunch, and make a bedtime snack. People can take pride in the cakes they bake.

Next, a fine home has a clock. People use clocks to get the time. Some clocks chime to help them wake up. It is rude to be late for a plane, a game, or a date! A clock's size is not important. Big clocks and little clocks can all do the same fine job! My small clock wakes me at nine!

What home lacks a sink and a tub? A fine home has a spot for people to take a bath. It also has a spot to scrub pots, pans, dishes, glasses, teeth, and hands!

Another thing a fine home includes is light. The light can shine in from a big window. It can also come from a bulb in a bedside lamp or a desk lamp. But in a storm, you might have to use a flashlight!

To finish, what is a home without a bed? A fine home can include many kinds of beds. The beds can be bunk beds, twin beds, wide beds, cribs, and cots. A bed is a fine spot to take a nap, read a book, and listen to a tune!

Words with long *i*, long *u*

bedside	five	like	prune	size	use
bedtime	fine	likes	rude	time	used
chime	include	nine	shine	tune	wide
dine	includes	pride			

High Frequency Words

all	from	make	next	same	use
come	home	many	people	small	without
family					

Decodable Passage 17

Spike Escapes

I have a pet snake. His name is Spike. Spike lives in a big glass tank in my bedroom, and I give him mice to eat. I think snakes make great pets, but my mother doesn't. She has one strict rule. Spike must be in his tank all the time. I follow that rule, but sometimes Spike does not. Last night, he got out of his tank. I knew I had to find him before Mom did. Spike is quite big, so I didn't think that would be a problem. But it was—it was a big problem!

I bent down and felt around in the dark closet. I gave something a poke, but it was just a sock. Under the bed I saw one skate, two dimes, three cubes from a game, and five pens, but no snake.

I looked in the kitchen cabinets behind plates, cups, glasses, and a box of cake mix. Then I searched inside the stove, under the table, and in a spot next to the mops.

In the bathroom, I looked in the tub and under piles of towels. Under the sink, I just saw a thick black and white striped pipe. Then I thought about that. The pipe under the sink isn't striped—it's white. Spike has stripes—that was a snake on the pipe! I learned my lesson. When I put him back in his tank, I set a large rock on the tank's mesh top. Spike will not escape again very soon!

Words with long *a*, long *o*, long *i*, long *u*

cake	game	named	poke	snake	striped
cubes	gave	piles	quite	snakes	stripes
dimes	inside	pipe	rule	Spike	time
escapes	make	plates	skate	stove	white
five					

High Frequency Words

all	find	make	out	three	under
down	from	mother	something	two	when
eat	large	one	sometimes		

Decodable Passage 18

Fun Time at Home

Time at home can be spent at work and play. As a rule, the work comes first, and then it's time for fun.

Jobs at home can be endless. In the winter, most jobs take place inside the home. All the people in a family can take part—both adults and kids. They can mop a floor until it shines. Even kids can scrub a tub and shake the dust out of rugs and drapes.

But even in winter, time at home is not just about work. There is time for fun games inside, such as jacks, chess, and "Go Fish." You can play a tune on a flute, sing a tune, or bake a batch of cupcakes. You can also go outside to slide on your sleds or skate on the ice.

Then in the spring, jobs can include things you do outside. In the bright sunshine, you can rake and dig a plot for plants. You can give your deck a rinse and then a new coat of paint. You can pick up all those sticks and branches that broke off the trees and rake them into a big pile.

But you can also have fun in the sun when it's hot! You can ride bikes, skate on the sidewalk, catch a ball, and fly a kite. You can make a grid on the pavement. Then get a rock or a stone and use it to play hopscotch. You can get a rope and jump rope with a pal.

Which activity do you like best when you have time at home?

Words with long *a*, long *i*

bake	games	kite	rake	shines	sunshine
bike	inside	pavement	ride	skate	take
cupcakes	make	pile	shake	slide	time
drapes					

High Frequency Words

all	first	make	people	use
come	go	new	then	when
family	home	out	there	

Decodable Passage 19

Far Away

"Some day," Ray tells Gail, "I plan to take a trip far, far away."

"Where will you go?" asks Gail.

"Maybe I will sail to Spain," says Ray. "I'd like to go this very day. Spain is way across the sea. It has big mountains and wide plains. I can play in Spain, if it does not rain very much. I will ride the subway and the fast train. I will stay until May. It will be a fine holiday."

"Can you go to Australia?" asks Gail. "That's even farther away than Spain."

"How can I get there?" Ray asks.

"You can take a plane, or you can sail," says Gail, "but you cannot take a train. Australia is a continent in the southern hemisphere. The mainland is a big island. You can play in the sand and hike on trails. You can stay for days and days, and you can mail me notes from there. You may get to play with a kangaroo that has a big tail!"

"That will be fun," says Ray, "but maybe I'll go even farther away."

"You don't say?" asks Gail.

"Yes, I just may aim for a trip to space," Ray says.

"That's great," says Gail, "but how will you get all that way?"

"I will find a way. I may ride a rocket ship."

"Explain how you will pay for your fun trip to space," Gail says.

"I will find a way," says Ray. "And, I just can't wait!"

Words with long *a* spelled *ai* and *ay*

aim	holiday	maybe	rain	Spain	trails
away	mail	pay	Ray	stay	train
day	mainland	plains	sail	subway	wait
explain	May	play	say	tail	way
Gail					

High Frequency Words

all	from	or	says
find	go	say	there

Decodable Passage 20

Six Tips Before You Leave

Let's say that you must pack for a trip that will last a week, and your goal is to take only a big backpack. What will you take? These six tips can show you how to squeeze everything that you need in just one backpack. Have faith. You won't fail. It will be a real breeze!

Tip 1 Make a list of the things you need. Greed can make you pack too much! Don't take a load of stuff you don't need. Match things that go together. Ask yourself: Will I use that yellow jacket? Will I really need three sweatshirts in that heat?

Tip 2 Wear the big stuff. Don't pack a coat—wear it. Slip on those jeans, too. Jeans take up a lot of room in a backpack.

Tip 3 Be neat, and don't just throw stuff in. Roll up things like socks, jackets, and pants. Clothes take up much less space when they're rolled, not folded.

Tip 4 Take some laundry soap, and use it to wash your things while you're away. It takes just ten seconds to soak your pants and tops to get them clean. Then you can wear each thing two or three times.

Tip 5 Each pair of shoes takes up a lot of space in a backpack. Pack just one extra set of shoes, not more. Your feet won't mind a bit!

Tip 6 Take your time as you pack. Don't just throw things in the bottom of the backpack. If you rush, you will end up with things that you don't need on the trip.

Now that you know these tips for how to pack, it's time to load up your backpack and go!

Words with long *o* spelled *oa, ow*					
coat	load	soak	soap	throw	yellow
goal	show				

Words with long *e* spelled *ea, ee*					
breeze	feet	jeans	neat	real	three
clean	greed	leave	need	squeeze	week
each	heat				

High Frequency Words				
go	more	really	then	two
leave	one	say	three	use
make	or	second	together	when

Decodable Passage 21

Camp in the Snow

It's fun to backpack in the summer, but it's great to backpack when it snows! You can see nature like never before. A hush blankets the trails, and the landscape is so white that it gleams.

When you know how to camp, it is a treat to camp in the snow. But, you must know what to bring. Let me teach you how to beat the cold. When the wind blows, it can feel well below zero degrees. Cold can make a dream trip become a nightmare!

Don't leave home without a coat that keeps out the rain and snow. Coats made of down, or goose feathers, keep in heat so hikers can feel as warm as toast! Waterproof boots help, too. Special heels and soles protect the feet to make a hike fun and safe.

A hiker needs to sleep well. A warm sleeping bag is a must so you won't freeze. The best bags are filled with down. It is always painful to sleep on the ground. A thick foam pad beneath the bag will help.

It is important to eat well when you camp. You just can't beat a small gas stove. It can heat water for hot drinks like tea. You can prepare hot meals by pouring hot water into a bag that contains dried food. The sealed bags contain many different treats, like cheese, milk, beans, peas, grains, and meat. Just unseal the bag, and add water. Be sure to throw some G.O.R.P. in your backpack. G.O.R.P is a sweet treat made from good old raisins and peanuts!

So, if you want to camp and hike in the snow on your next holiday, plan away! You will not regret it!

Words with long e spelled ee, ea; long a spelled ai, ay; long o spelled oa, ow

always	coat	freeze	leave	raisins	teach
away	contains	gleams	meals	sealed	throw
beans	degrees	grains	meat	see	toasts
beat	dream	heat	needs	sleep	trails
below	eat	heels	painful	sleeping	treat
beneath	feel	holiday	peanuts	snow	treats
blows	feet	keep	peas	sweet	unseal
cheese	foam	keeps	rain	tea	

High Frequency Words

always	down	important	next	want
below	eat	leave	or	water
by	from	many	out	when
different	home	make	small	without

Decodable Passage 22

Sailing Ships

The ship glides through the water and up to the dock. The sails flap and groan as the boat slows down, as if to protest the landing. Teens tie the vessel with ropes. Mothers and fathers wait ten feet away. Each student is greeted with a smile. The teens seem relaxed as the ship reaches the coast.

Each spring, at least 40 students sail ships on the open sea with SEA, Sea Education Association. In a lab at sea, students study fish, plankton, sea plants, and the sea itself. The teens finish the course at the end of May. By then, they have grown to love the sea.

Sailing can be difficult at times. The students had to clean the sailboat once a day. They had to scrub the decks and shine the brass railings each week. They helped prepare all the food for each meal.

Each day, a team of students had to keep watch for six hours. Being on watch was demanding. A student had to take the wheel and make sure the boat stayed on course. A helmsman had to pay attention each second. One mistake could mean a real problem.

Students had to watch for boats within three miles away. Between sunset and sunrise, students had to take turns looking for boats on the horizon.

By the end of the trip at sea, each student had learned to sail a huge ship, raise the main sails, and name 200 rope knots. These teens can say they are real sailors.

Words with long *e* spelled *ee*, *ea*; long *a* spelled *ai*, *ay*; long *o* spelled *oa*, *ow*

away	each	main	reaches	say	team
between	feet	May	real	sea	teens
boat	greeted	meal	sail	seamen	three
boats	groan	mean	sailboat	seem	wait
clean	grown	pay	sailing	slows	week
coast	keep	railings	sails	stayed	wheel
day	least	raise			

High Frequency Words

all	learned	mother	open	study	through
by	love	once	say	then	watch
down	make	one	second	three	water
father					

Decodable Passage 23

They Hiked at a Lake

Mack and Zack liked to take long hikes at a lake. One of the best paths was at the west end of the lake. There, they hiked past a big grove of pine trees. Mack collected pinecones. He used them to make gifts for his mom and dad.

The next best path at the lake was the east end. There the boys hiked up a big hill. Zack collected rocks. He used them to line the paths at his home. His dad liked the way the stones looked along the paths.

One day, Mack and Zack needed a change. This time, they hiked past the big lake. They looked for pinecones but did not find any. They looked for rocks to collect but did not find pretty stones. They stopped to look at frogs as they jumped in the reeds. They looked at ducks as they dived in the water. They gazed at a stream as it flowed into the lake.

At three, Mack and Zack went home. Zack's dad asked about stones for his paths. Mack's mom asked to see more pinecones. Then the boys told Mack's mom and Zack's dad about the things they saw at the lake. Mack's mom said that friends were better than gifts and stone paths. Zack's dad agreed.

Words with verb ending -ed

asked	dived	gazed	jumped	needed	used
collected	flowed	hiked	liked	stopped	

High Frequency Words

about	long	next	saw	three	water
find	make	one	then	use	were
home	more	said	there	was	

Decodable Passage 24

Bright Dogs

Do you know a person that cannot see well? If you do, you might know a service dog, too. This is a dog that helps people with bad sight. A helping dog can do many things to help these people. He tries to see just what the person needs. A helping dog is a real friend to the sight impaired.

Sight dogs are very bright animals. A sight dog can help someone get around. The dog knows the right way to go. Just tie a tight harness on the dog, and he will lead you on the right path. The dog will stop if it is not safe to cross a street. Then he will go when it is safe.

If a person needs to get a box from a high shelf, a helping dog tries with all his might to reach it. If the dog hears even a slight sound at night, he will bark to tell his owner about it. A sight dog might even switch on a light—no lie!

A sight dog tries his best to please his owner. He wants to do the right thing all the time. And it does not take much to reward the dog. He might sit upright and put his paw on your thigh just to get a pat on the head or a small treat. Then he sighs with delight. He knows that he did just the right thing.

Words with long *i* spelled *ie*

lie	tie	tries

Words with long *i* spelled *igh*

bright	light	night	sighs	slight	tight
delight	might	right	sight	thigh	upright
high					

High Frequency Words

sound

Decodable Passage 25

Rescue Teams

Rescue teams are the best! Rescue teams come when a person needs help. A rescue team brings tools to help. Rescue teams use boats, trucks, and even planes in their jobs. Rescue teams wear suits that keep them safe. A rescue team tries to do its job each day of the week.

If you get stuck on a high cliff or in a tight spot, a rescue team can help. The rescue team might bring equipment like ropes to save you. If you are on a cruise ship and the ship runs out of fuel, a rescue team might bring fuel to fill the fuel tank. If a car quits on a street full of trucks, a rescue team might push the car off the road and away from traffic.

Men and women on rescue teams know just what to do. Don't disagree with a rescue team when they come to help. Do just what the rescue team tells you to do. Then you will be in good hands. A rescue team will not fail to tell you the right thing.

Rescue teams continue with their jobs each day. They help people in need no matter what. You can depend on rescue teams. People value rescue teams because they make life safe. If you know someone on a rescue team, tell the person that you are glad he or she does that job. It is good to feel so safe!

Words with long *u* spelled *ui*

cruise   suits

Words with long *u* spelled *ue*

continue   fuel   rescue   value

High Frequency Words

life

Decodable Passage 26

Out of Harm's Way

Karl loves to teach kids how to be safe. Karl went on a walk and thought about many things that could harm kids.

Inside their houses, kids can slip on wet floors. Sharp knives can cut a kid's hand. Kids can trip on cords or rugs in the dark. Karl says, "Think smart to stay safe at home. Never run on wet floors. Switch on a bright light at night. Stay away from sharp knives and tools."

Karl went to a park. Most kids like to play in parks and backyards. Karl tells kids how to stay safe in parks and yards. Karl says, "Don't play with strange dogs. If a dog starts to bark, march away."

Kids can be harmed in a park when they ride bikes or play sports. Karl says, "Pads should be worn when you ride bikes or play sports. A hard fall can harm you." Sometimes, cars drive past fast. Karl says, "On the way to the park, listen for horns, and wait for the cars to pass. At the park, play far away from busy streets."

Kids need to know how to be safe in a storm. Trees might drop sharp branches that can cut an arm. A bad cut will leave a mark or a scar. Karl says, "To stay safe, stay inside during a storm."

Karl helps a lot of kids.

Words with *r*-controlled vowels spelled *ar*

arm	dark	harmed	march	parks	smart
backyards	far	harm's	mark	scar	starts
bark	hard	Karl	park	sharp	yards
cars	harm				

Words with *r*-controlled vowels spelled *or*

horns	or	sports	storm	worn

High Frequency Words

house	know	never	should

Decodable Passage 27

Teens Who Serve

It is not true that guys and girls who are teens don't care. No, sir! Just look around, and you will see teens that serve night and day, often for no pay.

First, a girl named Gert works as a clerk in a pet shelter. She is there day after day. Dirt on her skirt is okay with her. She loves cats and dogs. But, she loves bats, snakes, and birds that chirp, too. She believes they all deserve warm beds, fresh food to eat, and fresh water to stop their thirst. Her best T-shirt says, "I Support Animals!"

Then a boy named Kirk thinks about fir trees a lot. He even thinks of fir trees that grow in far-away parts of the world. He works hard to help preserve old fir forests. The shirt I will get him for his birthday will say, "Fir Trees First!"

Third, my sister helps a doctor for no pay. She squirts liquid cleaner day after day. No dirt is left behind after she gets through! Her motto is, "Get Stern with Dirt!"

And last, teams of teens work on trails in parks. They clean the trails where people hike all day. They sweep rocks off to the side. Their shirts may say, "Save Our Parks!"

Today's teens deserve a lot of praise for their hard work. They serve us in so many ways. They make the world a better place. Let's pay them with our praise. We should give teens like Gert, Kirk, and my sister a pat on the back.

Words with *r*-controlled vowels spelled *er*

better	clerk	Gert	preserve	sister	stern
cleaner	deserve	her	serve		

Words with *r*-controlled vowels spelled *ir*

birds	dirt	girl	shirts	squirts	thirst
birthday	fir	girls	sir	third	T-shirt
chirp	first	Kirk	skirt		

High Frequency Words

often	should

Decodable Passage 28

Be Fair to Bears

Bears are big solid mammals with strong legs, long noses, short tails, and thick fur. Bears are the same kind of animals as seals and walruses.

Despite their large size and lumbering walk, bears have a flair for swimming and scaling trees. Sharp claws help bears grip and tear. Bears are active during the evenings. Their sharp sense of smell helps them navigate and find food.

A bear's diet includes fish, insects, rodents, and grasses. Bears also eat scraps that people leave behind at campsites. Bears don't spend much time in pairs. They prefer to live and hunt alone.

Bears survive the cold, harsh winters by sleeping. They shelter themselves in caves or dens and hibernate until spring returns. They don't eat, drink, or wake the entire winter. When spring arrives, starving bears come out of their lairs to hunt.

Your favorite teddy bear may be soft and sweet, but real bears can be very threatening. Female bears defend their cubs at all costs. People have taken over much of the bear's natural habitat, leaving bears little room to roam free. Laws have been passed to protect bears' habitats and give them a fair chance at survival.

Bears often perform in traveling shows. Trained bears may wear costumes or perform feats such as standing on chairs, walking across wires, or twirling. Many think making bears perform stunts and tricks is unfair. Bears are not stuffed dolls. They need fresh air and room to roam. Be fair. Let bears run free. Pick up litter. Keep the bear's habitat clean!

Words with *r*-controlled vowels spelled *air, ear*

air	chairs	flair	lairs	tear	wear
bears	fair	hair	pairs	unfair	

High Frequency Words

also	been	often

Decodable Passage 29

Be a Volunteer

At times, do you wish you could make this planet a better home for everyone? If so, maybe you can be a volunteer and donate time to helping others.

If you can't think of the kinds of things to do as a volunteer, look for projects near your home, such as at a school or a church. Ask your mom and dad to tell you when they hear of a project that you might like.

There are lots of things a kid can do as a volunteer. If you prefer being in nature, help clean up the shoreline of a lake, bay, or river, or volunteer in a wildlife shelter. Maybe you will help heal a sick bird or help a deer with a broken leg.

Perhaps you have a clear talent for music or art. If so, offer to help teach these skills to other kids. You can volunteer each year on Thanksgiving to prepare supper and cheer up the homeless.

Helping in any way is important. Don't be afraid that you lack the skills to be a volunteer. Mentors will be grateful and glad to teach you the things you need to know. And be proud as a volunteer! Peers may sneer when you say that you work hard for no pay, but just tell them that the sheer joy of giving is enough payment.

Words with *r*-controlled vowels spelled *ear, eer*

cheer	deer	hear	peer	sneer	year
clear	fear	near	sheer	volunteer	

High Frequency Words

could	know

120 Decodable Passages

© NGSP & HB

Decodable Passage 30

Penny Candy

It is funny to think about life in the years before we were born. My great granddad told me that many types of candy were a penny when he was young. Things were different then—candy was cheap, but life was hard.

In those years, there were more farms and fewer stores. People on farms had to make most of the items they needed by hand. They stitched quilts, spun wool into yarn, and made berry or peach jelly and saved it for the winter. Cows provided milk for butter, cheese, and yogurt. Hens gave eggs, and two big oxen joined with a yoke pulled a plow to prepare the rocky land for crops. Each day, whether sunny, windy, or rainy, the whole family got up at sunrise to work.

Today, things sound easy compared to then. We don't ride for days in horse-pulled carts along bumpy, dusty roads. We can fly in planes and arrive in much less time. Today, we might have a puppy in a yard rather than an ox in a field.

My great granddad missed the open sky of the farm. He joked that there was plenty of fresh air for everyone back on the farm.

I am happy to have the things that modern life offers us. We're lucky that we can buy jelly or yogurt instead of having to make it by hand. Would I go back in time to visit an old farm if I could? Sure, why not! But just for a visit.

Words with *y*

berry	dusty	jelly	puppy	types	yarn
bumpy	easy	lucky	rainy	why	years
by	fly	my	rocky	windy	yogurt
candy	funny	penny	sky	yard	yoke
day	happy	plenty	sunny		

High Frequency Words

along	before	life	much	why
back	could	miss	sound	would

Decodable Passage 31

Pointers from an Employed Mom

When I was a boy, my mother went back to work and my dad stayed at home. Mom worried that we would not survive without her, so she left us reminders … everywhere!

Inside the cupboard, a note said, "TOO MANY SNACKS WILL SPOIL DINNER." In the refrigerator, notes on the sirloin steaks said, "FOR DINNER," on the green beans, "PLEASE BOIL," and on the soy sauce, "FOR SALTY FLAVOR." A note that said, "USE FOIL IN THE PAN WHEN YOU BROIL THE MEAT" was on the stove. The same note was in the drawer with the foil.

On the back door were three notes: for Dad to remember to oil the squeaking hinge, for me to coil the hose after watering the garden, and for all of us to wipe the soil off our feet before coming inside.

When she ran out of short reminders to point out on notes, she began to send postcards with more details. She told my sister to avoid waiting until late to do homework. She sent me one to say not to annoy my sister or make too much noise, and to help her with homework. She even sent a postcard to the dog! She asked him to please just chew his toys instead of destroying the furniture.

I missed my mom when she went back to work, but with all the notes, it was like she was still there … everywhere!

Words with diphthongs and variant vowels spelled *oi, oy*					
annoy	boy	destroying	noise	pointers	soy
avoid	broil	employed	oil	sirloin	spoil
boil	coil	foil	point	soil	toys

High Frequency Words					
back	but	much	oil	until	would
before					

Decodable Passage 32

How to Speak "Cow"

Most of the time, we speak to say things with words. But sometimes we express feelings in other ways. A frown or pout can mean "I'm unhappy." A smile or shout may show joy. But what about an animal? How does it tell us its feelings? How does it tell another animal how it feels? It uses more than just its mouth!

Animals may use sounds or movements to communicate. You may have a dog or cat in your house. Can you tell when it is content or upset? Does the cat bound to the door to show it is happy to see you? Does the dog growl when you take away its bone? When your cat drops a mouse at your feet, it may meow to say that it is proud of this gift.

Animals that dwell outside may communicate better with other animals than with humans. Researchers have found that the sound a cow makes can tell other cows its age, whether it is male or female, and how it ranks in the herd. To find their rank, cows may butt their heads together to see who is stronger.

Water fowl like ducks and geese call to each other as they prepare to fly. A loud call can mean the bird is excited or angry. The calls are distinct if the bird is in the air flying or down on the ground.

Animals can say a lot without words. If we open our ears and eyes, they may teach us a lot.

Words with diphthongs and variant vowels spelled *ou*, *ow*

about	down	frown	how	mouth	shout
bound	foul	ground	loud	outside	sound
cow	fowl	growl	meow	pout	sounds
cows	found	house	mouse	proud	without

High Frequency Words

as	but	found	house	sound	words
away	each				

Decodable Passage 33

The View from Space

Major Cooper looked out the window at the view below. The Earth gleamed like wet dew on a very large jewel. Thin wisps of clouds floated by a yellow moon.

The major squeezed the stuffed kangaroo that Lewis gave her before she left. Suddenly, she missed her two boys. Her crew's mission was good for her career. Still, sometimes it was hard to be away from her kids. It seemed like they grew like bamboo shoots while she was away. Soon, she would be home.

Major Cooper turned on her computer and saw that she had a new message. She hooted when she saw that it was an e-mail from Lewis.

Dear Mom,

We hope you have a blast in space. It's so cool that you could go.

Tonight we think we saw your space craft. It wasn't a star, because it did not blink. It wasn't a planet, either. IT HAD TO BE YOU!

We miss you so much, but Dad has been taking good care of us. We have not had one fast food meal yet. (Boo hoo!) Dad made stew, and we couldn't chew it!

Boots got into real trouble. We went to the beach today. Boots got loose and ate a rotten fish, or maybe a crab. It stank! None of us would let her kiss us after that! We had to shampoo her when we got home.

It's time for bed. We send you big hugs and hope you have a smooth trip.

Lewis

Words with diphthongs and variant vowels spelled *oo, ew*					
bamboo	Cooper	grew	Lewis	stew	smooth
Boo hoo	crew	hooted	loose	shampoo	soon
Boots	dew	jewel	moon	shoots	view
chew	food	kangaroo	new		

High Frequency Words					
away	been	but	into	miss	seemed
because	before	could	made	much	would

Decodable Passage 34

Reptile Jigsaws

Dinosaurs were reptiles, the same type of animals as snakes, lizards, and turtles. They came in all shapes and sizes. Some were tall, and some were small. Some had sharp teeth and claws. Their bones help us find out about these reptiles that lived in the past.

After scientists dig up the bones, they must set them together like a jigsaw puzzle. This isn't an easy job because many bones may be missing or broken. At times, there may be just one or two bones, like an arm bone or a jaw fragment.

Scientists study the parts they find. They check the teeth to see how the dinosaur chewed its food. They study the leg bones to see how it walked. Then they work in teams to make the jigsaw puzzle. Artists draw what the reptile may have looked like. They craft the missing bones from glass and install bolts to join all the parts. The finished puzzle is a model of what the real dinosaur looked like.

The puzzle may end up with flaws because no one has seen a real dinosaur. But if you pause and study a display about them, there is still so much you can learn.

We may never find out what these extinct reptiles looked like, but the jigsaw puzzles show us a lot. We can tell which ones glided like hawks or were as harmless as fawns. It's interesting and fun to learn as much as we can about the past.

Words with diphthongs and variant vowels spelled *au, aw; al, all*

all	Dinosaurs	flaws	jaw	pause	tall
because	draw	hawks	jigsaw	small	walked
claws	fawns	install	jigsaws		

High Frequency Words

| as | because | but | lived | much | never |

Decodable Passage 35

Dance Practice

Grace sat at the table as Mom diced celery and added it to the rice in the pot. Grace looked concerned, so Mom asked why she had a worried face. "I want to audition for the dance team," Grace said, "but I can't do the fast steps. The song has a fast pace, and I have a hard time keeping up."

"Maybe you just have to practice some more," Mom said as she added spices to the rice. "Why don't you call Pam? She is on the city dance team. I bet she can watch you and give you some good advice."

"Great plan, Mom!" Grace said. "I'll ask her tomorrow."

After school the next day, Pam came to Grace's house. She helped Grace practice her dance steps. When Grace rushed to keep up with the pace, Pam slowed her down. "It's not a race!" she said. "Make each step precise. You'll get faster as you learn the steps."

Grace practiced with Pam after school twice a week. As she learned the steps, she made sure to place her feet just right. Finally, it was time to audition. Grace did her best. After all her practice, keeping the pace was easy, just like Pam said it would be.

On Friday, the list of girls who made the dance team was posted. Grace's name was on the list. She had made the dance team! She called Mom.

"Your hard work paid off!" Mom said in an excited voice. "I'll cancel my meeting. Let's pick up Pam and go get some ice cream to celebrate!"

Words with soft c

advice	city	excited	pace	precise	spices
cancel	concerned	face	place	race	twice
celebrate	dance	Grace	practice	rice	voice
celery	diced	ice			

High Frequency Words

as	but	each	made	why	would
asked	called	house			

Decodable Passage 36

A Gem of Advice

Bruce was not good at winning races or contests of any kind. He lost almost all the challenges he entered.

"Another contest?" Ginger asked. "I don't think you've noticed, but you're no ace at winning. You'll lose for sure."

"You don't know that," Bruce answered. "It sounds strange, but even when I finish in last place, I learn something that I can change next time."

"What did you learn when you lost the road race?" Ginger asked.

"I learned that I had to check my shoe laces so I wouldn't trip and fall," Bruce answered. "So I made sure to check my laces in my next race."

"But you didn't win that race either!" Ginger said. "Your pace was too slow. You lost by a huge margin."

"You're right, I didn't win. But I learned that I had to practice more. And I practiced a lot for the dance contest. I was so graceful."

Ginger cringed. "Was that the time you fell off the stage and hurt your face?"

"Yes," Bruce admitted, "and my leg, too. I wore a bandage and a brace for six weeks. But I bounced back, and I learned something. Now I stay in the center of the stage when I dance."

"I'll win this time," said Bruce. "It will be a cinch. I just need to use everything I've learned since I was young!"

And that's when Bruce won his first contest.

"Any gem of advice?" the principal asked Bruce as he handed him a huge medal.

"Gee, yes. Just keep trying!" Bruce said with a giant grin.

Words with soft *g*

challenge	cringed	exchanging	Ginger	large	strange
change	exchange	gem	huge		

High Frequency Words

another	learn	said	something	wouldn't	young
answered	now				

A Gem on Ice

Sage got her first pair of ice skates when she was very young. She loved the ice like mice love cheese. On the ice, her face lit up in a huge smile. Her eyes lit up, too. "This is my place!" she thought. Time on ice was a magic time. Her urge to skate was huge! And she skated with grace. "You are a gem on ice," her mother and father said.

One day, Sage said, "I want to learn to do something new. I want to learn to ice dance. It is all the rage. This is my choice. When I am on the ice, I am at peace. It is like being on a stage." Her mother and father thought it was a great idea.

Now, here she was at the finals. She laced up her skates and thought, "This is my chance to take charge." She forced herself to smile as she glided onto the ice in front of the large crowd.

Sage took her place in the center of the ice rink. Gems shone from her costume. The people in the crowd ceased clapping. She gave a nod, and her music started.

Sage moved with grace along the ice. She leaned into her first jump. She twirled around once, twice, and landed on her blade. "Perfect!" she thought, as she glided on. She braced herself for the next jump. It was an important one, and it would count a lot with the judges. She forced herself to concentrate. Then she spun and leaped into space! The noise of the crowd told her that she had aced the jump.

The judges held up their cards: 10, 10, 10! This was Sage's best dance ever!

Words with soft g spelled g					
charge	gems	large	rage	stage	urge
gem	huge	magic	Sage		

Words with soft c spelled c					
aced	center	dance	grace	mice	space
braced	chance	face	ice	peace	twice
ceased	choice	forced	laced	place	

High Frequency Words					
along	ever	idea	into	now	would
as					

Decodable Passage 38

A Summer by the Brook

Jon and Les were very different. Jon preferred to be in the woods, and Les loved reading books inside. They were both having a lonely summer. Every day, Jon took his fishing rod and hooks and went alone to the brook in the woods. Sometimes he sat on a log to catch fish, and sometimes he stood on a rock. Most of the fish were too small, so he would unhook them and throw them back. While Jon was in the woods, Les sat inside all day in a window nook and read good books. It was the only place he liked to sit and read because he could look out the window.

When their father saw that they never spent time together, he shook his head with dismay. He understood that his sons were different, but he was sad that they would spend so much of their childhood apart. "Look, boys," he said. "Why don't we do something together? Why don't we build something that you can both use and enjoy?"

So, they all went to the lumberyard to buy wood. Les went to the library to find books on carpentry while Jon and his dad took the tools out of the basement. Together, the three of them worked hard to build a new bench. It was a beautiful bench, and they put it in the woods near the brook. It was big enough for both Jon and Les to sit on. Jon fished while Les read aloud from books about fish and other creatures in the brook. The brothers spent the rest of the summer together. On the back of the bench, they painted the words, "Built by Jon and Les—Brothers and Good Friends."

Words with variant vowels spelled oo

books	good	nook	stood	understood	wood
brook	hooks	shook	took	unhook	woods
childhood	look				

High Frequency Words

back	could	much	put	why	would
because	friends	never	while	words	

Decodable Passage 39

Design for Recovery

It was a snowstorm for the ages. Jami Goldman drove home from a skiing trip in the mountains, when she took a wrong turn. Hours later, she was stuck in a snowstorm for days. After many days, she and her friend were rescued, but then she got some bad news from the doctors. She lost both her legs to frostbite. They were amputated below both knees.

Being an amputee was not something Jami had ever thought about. She was only in her twenties, and her whole life loomed ahead. She knew she had to work hard. The first thing she did was go to college to get a degree. Then she started to race.

Like many amputees, Jami was fitted with artificial limbs. When she raced on a track, she used special legs called "Cheetahs." They cost $3,000, but they gave her freedom to become what she wanted—an athlete and a competitor.

Not content to just run races, Jami wrote a book about her life called "Up and Running." She tells about being stuck in the snowstorm and how she worked to make herself strong again. Her story inspires anyone who has ever had problems. Her life is a design for recovery.

Words with variant vowels and consonants spelled *gn, kn*; *wr*; *dge*; *mb*					
design	knees	knew	limbs	wrong	wrote

High Frequency Words					
but	ever	life	mountains	news	story
called					

This is not a good day!

Short *a* and Short *o*

A Bad Day!

Words with /ă/*a*; /ŏ/*o*			
am	class	lot	tan
and	dad	mad	van
at	ham	mom	
bad	has	not	
bag	hot	sad	
can	jog	stops	

High Frequency Word
home

© NGSP & HB

I am at lunch at 12:00. I have hot ham. I do not like ham. I am sad and mad.

I am at school at 8:00.

I have a class at 8:15. I do not have my tan bag. My tan bag is at home.

I jog a lot in P.E. I am hot! I stop.

6   **3**

Mom is mad. Mom can
not come. Dad can.

Dad stops the van.
Dad has my tan bag.

4

5

It is such a mess! Mom does not like it a bit. Jim just grins.

Catch, Mom!

Short *i*, Short *u*, *ch*, and *tch*

Words with /ĭ/*i*; /ŭ/*u*; /ch/*ch*, tch			
bag	fills	it	stuff
big	grabs	Jim	such
bit	grins	just	switch
bunch	hits	much	will
but	hunts	pop	
catch	in	rip	
fast	is	snack	

High Frequency Words		
open	then	there

Jim hits the TV switch.

Popcorn fills the room fast!

Oh, no!

Jim looks at his snack. Jim can spot a rip in the bag. Jim opens the microwave.

Then Jim hunts for a snack. There is just a bunch of old stuff, but Jim does spot a bag of . . .

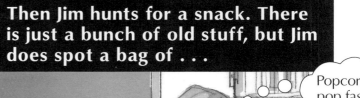

Popcorn! It will pop fast.

It will not take much time.

Jim grabs a bag. He does not spot a rip in the bag.

Jim can mix punch as it pops.

At last, the day ends. Mom has one last job for Fred.

Zzzzzzz

Fred! Help me carry these bags.

Where is Fred? He is in bed! Zzzzzzzz.

Short *e*, *sh*, *ck*, and Double Consonants

Fred at Work

Words with /ĕ/*e*; /sh/*sh*; /k/*ck*			
bed	Fred	mess	stack
chest	fresh	net	trash
docks	gets	picks	when
ends	help	shop	yes

High Frequency Words		
love	there	want

© NGSP & HB

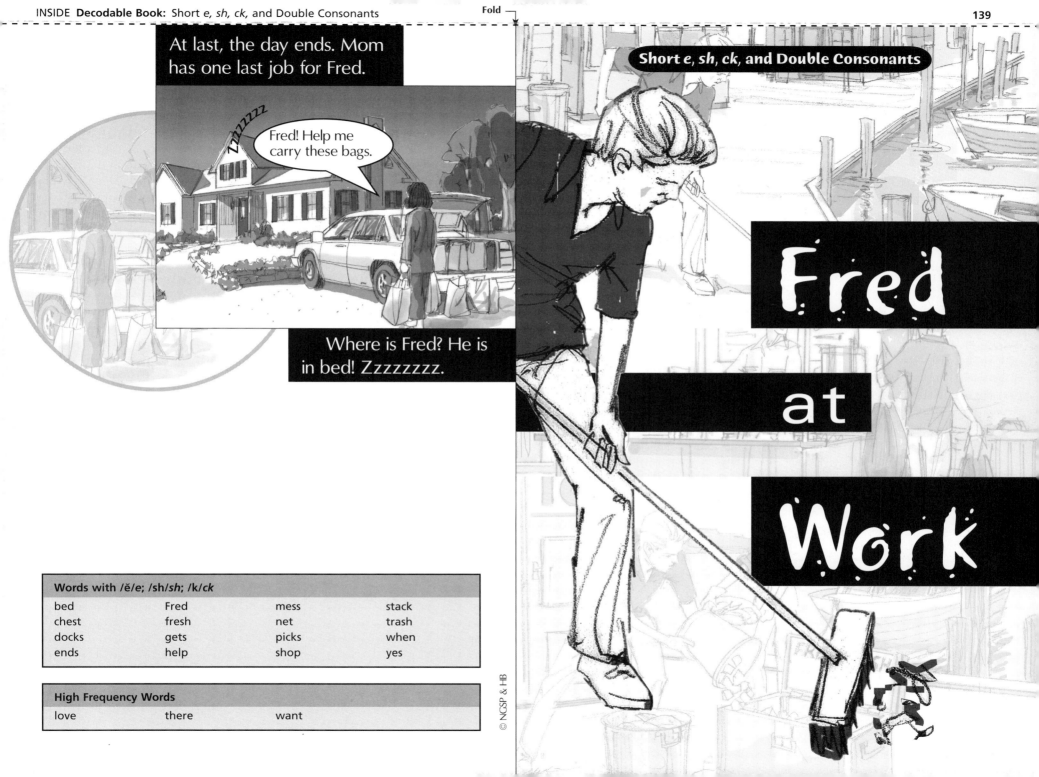

Fred loves his job on the docks.
Fred gets to help a lot.

Fred takes trash to a bin.

Jill has a batch of fresh fish.

I can help. I will fill the chest with ice.

ICE

FRESH FISH

Fred helps a girl get her hat.

THE LUNCH SPOT

I get a net for jobs like this.

That day, Fran runs at a track meet. But Fran is not last. Fran is first!

Run, Fran, run!

Blends and Digraphs

From Last to First

Words with Blends and Digraphs			
bang	from	ring	thinks
catch	kids	rush	track
check	last	sock	which
clock	left	spot	
fast	lunch	still	
Fran	pack	that	

High Frequency Words		
first	from	want

© NGSP & HB

We can't stop yet!

You go. I can't move. No more food festivals for me.

EXIT

Word Patterns and Multisyllabic Words

basket	happens	stand	crab
chips	hundreds	stands	sandwich
chopsticks	is	sum	has
dim	muffins	that	had
Ekram	napkin	this	
festival	Pedro	with	
fish	shish-ke-bob	pumpkin	

High Frequency Words

all	first	new	something
city	love	next	there
enough	more	people	want
find	move	second	

© NGSP & HB

Word Patterns and Multisyllabic Words

A City Food Festival

The city is a great place to be. Something new happens all the time.

What is this? There are hundreds of people here.

It's the city Food Festival. Come on, Pedro. Let's go!

Do you want a crab sandwich?

No! Not for me.

Pedro has had enough to eat.

Fold

Grandmother likes all the things we do for her. She even likes my brother's drums.

CRASH!

BANG!

Long Vowels: *a, i, o, u*

At Home

Words with Long Vowels: *a, i, o, u*			
cakes	hope	robe	tune
bake	like	smiles	use
fine	make	take	
home	notes	time	

High Frequency Words			
all	from	out	wants
down	her	together	
eat	our	something	

© NGSP & HB

My grandmother is here from Japan. Our family is glad to see her. We hope she likes our home.

Soon it is time to eat. We use our best dishes for the food. We take out the best glasses. Then we sit down and eat together. Grandmother smiles and smiles.

I like this food! The cake is good, too!

2

7

My mother makes crab rolls for Grandmother.

We really like these. I hope she will, too.

We want to make Grandmother glad that she came to see us. So we think of special things to do for her. In Japan, Grandmother does not bake cakes. So I make her one.

It smells good!

Long Vowels: *ai, ay; ee, ea; oa, ow* and Compound Words

It's the end of the day.

Well, we don't have any fish.

No, but we had a neat day, and it didn't rain!

On the
River

Words with Long Vowels: *ai, ay; ee, ea; oa, ow*			
cattail	deep	neat	toad
croak	eats	rain	weekend
day	hears	show	year
daytime	near	sleep	

High Frequency Words			
always	place	something	there
animals	river	small	water
one			

© NGSP & HB

Is that rain?

I don't think so.

In late June, Shane always spends a weekend with his granddad. This year Granddad takes him to Greenstone River. It's a good place to fish. You can also see a lot of wildlife there.

It's almost sunset. Still no fish. Shane asks if fish like this spot.

Fish like deep water. Once I caught a trout this big here.

Granddad knows the best places to find fish.

6

3

They wait for the fish to bite. While they wait, Shane sees something.

Shane hears something in the cattail plants.

4

5

Words with Verb Ending *-ed*			
hated	jogged	sailed	waited
hunted	played	stepped	

High Frequency Words			
about	animals	really	together
again	love	there	was
always	new	thought	were

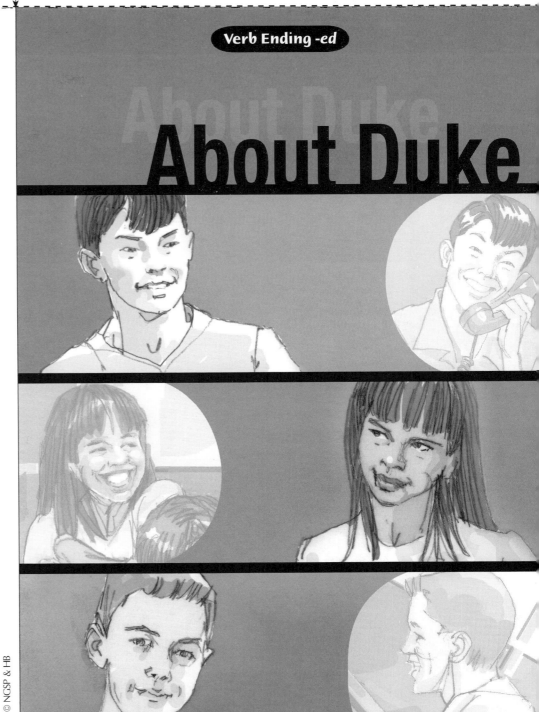

Verb Ending *-ed*

About Duke

6

3

Children are singing as we leave the fair. I look back, wondering if we really went into the past.

It's fun to celebrate the past this way!

Words with Verb Ending *-ing*			
beginning	joking	singing	thinking
dressing	pinning	slapping	throwing
eating	playing	taking	
getting	scrubbing	tasting	

High Frequency Words			
another	come	really	want
celebrate	people	something	young
city			

Verb Ending *-ing*

Celebrate the *Past*

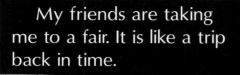

My friends are taking me to a fair. It is like a trip back in time.

This seems like a city in old England.

A play is beginning, and the actors are speaking to me! They ask me to come on the stage and be the queen!

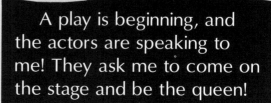

2   7

We are eating very odd food today. Todd is tasting something called "toad in the hole." I am feasting on "beef on a stick."

Do you need a bite to eat?

I am getting hungry!

People are dressing in costumes. We want to dress up, too. Sam has a velvet cap. Todd is pinning a ribbon on another hat.

Let's put on these hats.

Will this look good with braids?

They are playing tunes just like people played 400 years ago! A young man is twirling sticks.

Some women are scrubbing clothes in a stream. They are joking and slapping the cloth on rocks.

I like the way they talk.

I do, too. They speak the way people spoke long ago.

Long Vowels: *ie, igh; ui, ue*

RESCUE at the BEACH

Words with Long Vowels: *ie, igh; ui, ue*			
blue	high	right	suit
bright	might	sign	true
fight	rescue	skies	tried

High Frequency Words	
almost	never

This time, Ann listens. She does what Deb tells her.

Deb meets Ann and helps her to the shore.

The skies are blue and the water feels great. Ann and Kim plan to have a good day at the beach. They meet Deb on the sand.

Ann tries to fight the wave. Another high wave is coming. Deb yells to Ann. She tells Ann what to do.

Don't fight the wave! Let the next wave bring you in!

Ann is surprised that Deb is a lifeguard. Kim isn't.

I hope she never needs to rescue me.

It's true that Deb is small, but she is a really strong swimmer.

6

3

Ann is in a rush to get in the water and start surfing. She is between the waves and the rocks. She doesn't see the sign about the rocks. Deb tells her to watch out.

Ann doesn't listen to Deb. Then a big wave takes her close to the rocks. She needs help! Deb runs as fast as she can.

4   **5**

Teens Reach Out and Recycle

We need things for our yard sale NOW! Chairs, tools, games, skirts, shirts, French horns! Don't throw them away. We can use them! Call 555-9146.

Words with *R*-Controlled Vowels

art	curb	hurt	shirts
artist	dirt	March	skirts
barn	fern	Mark	star
Bert	first	market	start
birds	for	New York	third
car	hard	north	turn
chirp	homework	park	world
concert	horns	porch	yard

High Frequency Words

country	house	now

© NGSP & HB

Community Bulletin Board

All around the world, teens use their time and skills to help others. Teens in this country are no different. American teens use their skills to make the world a better place. Look around your city for a community bulletin board like the one on these pages. Find your own way to make a difference!

Start the Year Right!

Come and hear how to protect birds. Join **The Bird Group,** Sundays at 2:00 p.m., on the porch of The Country House, 524 Third Street (near Hassan's Market).

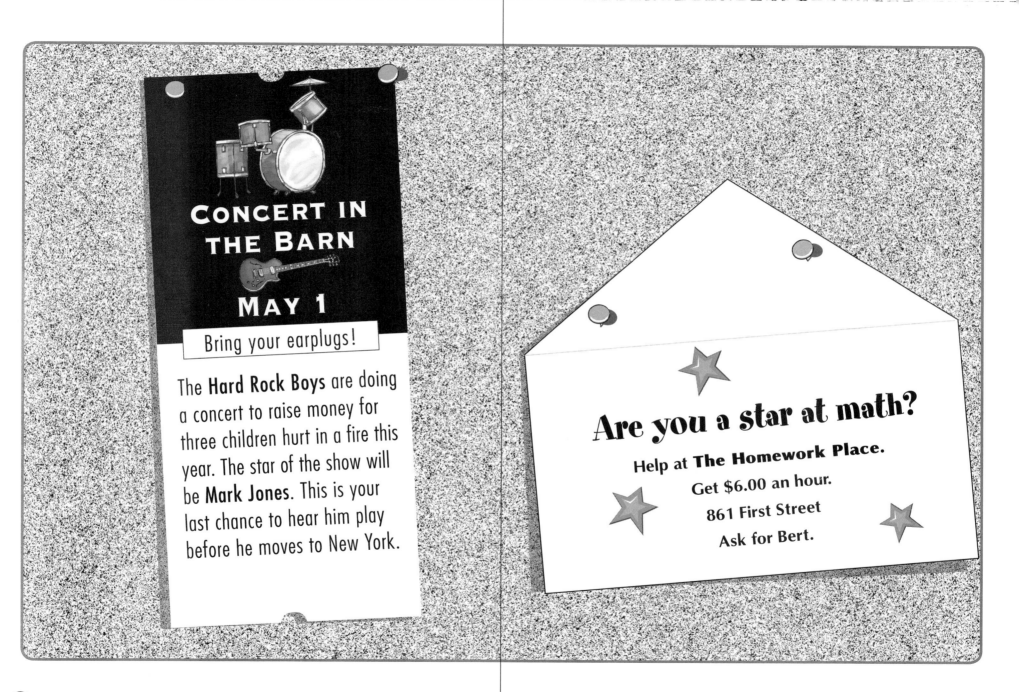

CONCERT IN THE BARN

MAY 1

Bring your earplugs!

The **Hard Rock Boys** are doing a concert to raise money for three children hurt in a fire this year. The star of the show will be **Mark Jones**. This is your last chance to hear him play before he moves to New York.

Are you a star at math?

Help at **The Homework Place.**

Get $6.00 an hour.

861 First Street

Ask for Bert.

Car Wash
$5.00
We get the dirt off!

Help our school band take a trip to Bear Mountain.

Bring your car to Park School, 10 Park Drive, on March 30.

(Go north on Fern Lane. Turn right on Park Drive. Park at the curb.)

Be an Artist for the Day
Make Art in the Park

March 31

You can **paint**. You can **weave** or make a **clay pot**. Funds will be used to add a room to Deerfield Senior Center.

The perfect moose may live for
as long as 12 years.

Words with *R*-Controlled Syllables		
antlers	member	under
expert	perfect	water
forests	swimmers	winter

High Frequency Words		
also	because	four
away	called	mountains

© NGSP & HB

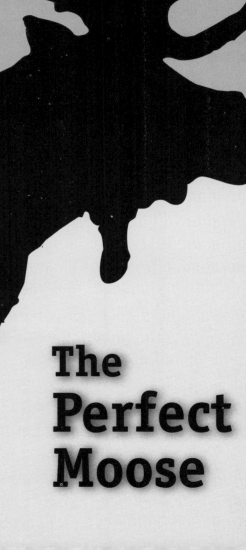

The Perfect Moose

elk

caribou

white-tailed deer

The moose is a member of the deer family. The white-tailed deer, the elk, and the caribou are part of this same family. Members of the deer family live in many parts of the world.

moose

A grown moose does not fear attack because it is so big. A wolf pack or a bear may attack a calf or a moose that is sick, but not one that is grown and strong.

wolf

brown bear

2

7

Moose live in northern mountains and forests. A mother is called a cow. A baby is called a calf. Calves are born in the spring and stay with the mother for a year. Then the mother chases them away, and they must survive on their own.

calf cow

Where moose live in North America

Moose like water and are expert swimmers. They wade in ponds and lakes to eat the plants that grow under the water. They also eat twigs and shrubs on land. Moose will not hunt animals, but some animals hunt them.

Moose like to live alone. They do not form herds like other members of the deer family. When there is a lot to eat, three or four moose may stay together for a while.

The male, or bull, has big antlers. He uses the antlers to fight other bulls during mating time. Bulls shed the antlers in the winter and grow new antlers in the spring.

antlers

hump

bell

4

5

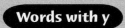

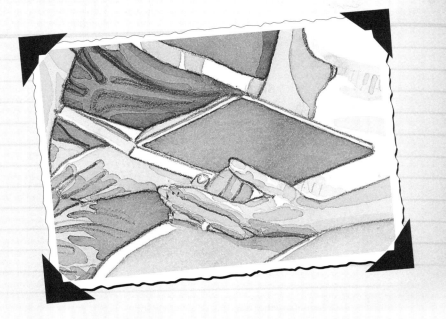

Kathy's

Diary

Words with *y*			
army	Grady	lucky	study
daddy	happy	my	
diary	Italy	silly	
entry	Kathy	sky	

High Frequency Words			
away	called	four	over
been	ever	life	words

© NGSP & HB

Back in 1945, Kathy Grady
started a diary. She wrote about
her life during that time.

Each page Kathy wrote is
called an entry. Here are some
entries from Kathy's diary.

In 1960, Kathy is all grown up.
She has two children of her own.
She reads her diary to them. Her
kids like to hear about life in the
1940s. It seems like a long time ago,
but the words in Kathy's diary bring
the past to life.

Daddy went to Italy three years ago. He is in the Army Air Force. He flies a big plane called a B-42.

My dad is home!

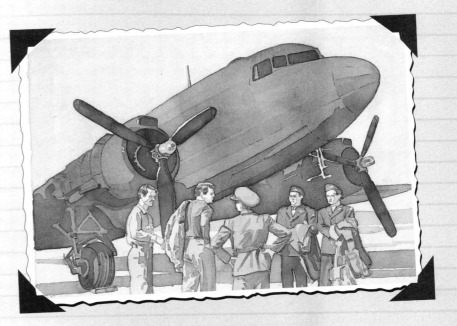

One of his Army buddies is with him. We feel so lucky to have him back! Mom is happier than ever. She is going to make french fries and hamburgers. They are Dad's favorite foods.

This picture shows my dad with some of his buddies. Dad is the second man on the right. We miss him so much!

Some nights we sit and study the sky. We are watching for our boys to fly home. Many of them have been away for four years!

People say the war may end soon! We all wait for that happy day.

The war is over! People are yelling and waving flags. You can hear their cries of joy. We all act silly. Mom is playing music and dancing.

I rushed out to get a newspaper. Dad can read it when he gets home.

The neighbors clapped with joy. At last, they all sat down to eat. They chatted and joked and ate lots of stew, just as they always did.

Enjoy!

The best ever!

Mmmm! Great stew!

Words with Diphthongs and Variant Vowels			
all	down	join	small
always	enjoy	joy	soon
awful	few	noon	stew
boiled	food	Paul	too
call	found	proud	town
called	frowned	salt	
crowd	house	saw	

High Frequency Words			
as	ever	house	made
called	few	into	over
each	found	lived	

Diphthongs and Variant Vowels

A Pinch of Salt

Once there was a wise woman named Mrs. Paul. She lived in a small house at the end of town. She was not rich, but all her neighbors loved her. One morning the woman saw that her cupboard was empty. She found only a few peas to eat. She was too proud to beg, but she was too smart to stay hungry.

She put the peas into the pot. She filled the pot with water. Then she put the pot over the fire, just as she always did.

It was time for the woman to add one last thing, just as she always did. She added a pinch of salt. She stirred the pot, then tasted the stew again.

Perfect!

The woman tasted
the stew. She frowned.

The neighbors smiled and
waited, just as they always did.

When the pot began
to simmer and steam, she
called to her neighbors.

All the neighbors heard her call.
They nodded and smiled, just as they
always did.

Soon, a crowd of neighbors entered her house. They each added food to the pot. They added carrots, meat, onions, and more peas. They filled the pot to the brim, just as they always did.

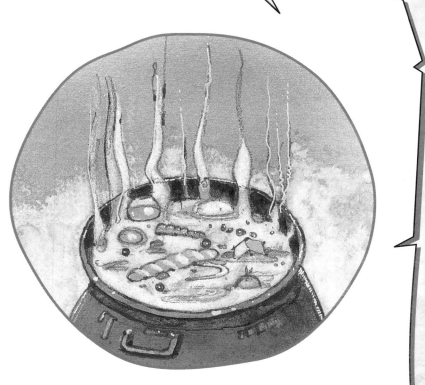

The pot boiled over the fire. By noon, the smell of rich stew filled the small house. It made the neighbors hungry.

4

5

He skates, and he falls. He falls, and he skates. He falls twice in a row, but he's such a good sport. Gene's friends knew he would have fun at hockey!

Can't I just hit the puck from here?

Sure!

Variant Vowels and Consonants

A Good Game

Mel   Gene   Rick

Words with Variant Vowels and Consonants			
cage	facemask	gives	huge
can't	game	going	ice
come	Gene	good	laces
edge	get	great	twice

High Frequency Words			
even	if	while	would
friends	into		

© NGSP & HB

Gene's friends take him to the ice rink to play hockey. There are kids on the ice already. They are playing a game. This is Gene's first time on skates.

I don't know about this!

Come on. You'll do fine!

We're your friends. We'll help you.

Gene looks at the other kids. They are moving so fast!

At last, Gene gets on the ice. He puts one foot in front of the other. He's on his feet, and he's skating!

The boys are ready to play. Mel shows Gene the puck. Rick gives him the wooden stick.

Gene does not think he will be good at hockey.

Gene sits at the edge of the ice. While he puts on his skates, he watches the players on the ice. Some of them are huge!

Mel wants to be sure Gene is safe.

Mel helps Gene strap on his shin guards. They will protect his knees and shins.

Strap the shin guards on tight.

Rick brings Gene some elbow pads.

Mel gives Gene a facemask.

Do I have to wear that?

Yes. You have to wear a facemask if you want to play.

Come on. It's a great game!

Rick can't wait to get in the game.

4

5

Last night we camped under a million stars! A coyote howled at the moon. Dad told funny stories about cowboys in the desert. I think we laughed for hours. I want to come back here soon.

See you next week. I have a lot of pictures to show you.

Multisyllabic Words			
amazing	cowboys	ladders	river
Anasazi	desert	midnight	skyscrapers
awake	Deven	music	stories
below	didn't	picture	thousands
border	dwellings	postcards	today
bridges	funny	rafting	towers
cabin	hiking	rapids	very
cooler	hundreds	reading	village
corners	jackets	relaxed	western

High Frequency Words			
back	even	miles	over
could	explore	million	states
country	high	mountains	until
four	house	much	walked
Earth	into	near	

Utah

Colorado

Four Corners

Arizona

New Mexico

Cabin near Flagstaff, Arizona

Hey, Brent! I am at Four Corners. This is the place where four states share a border. It is the only place in the U.S. like this. I stood on all four states at one time! Dad took a great picture of me.

I am reading a good book about the Anasazi. I could not put it down last night. I was awake until midnight!

Today, we just relaxed in our cabin. I was so tired. Dad got us big burritos for lunch.

There's a country-western music show later. I am going to dance and dance!

White Water Rafting in Arizona

This is the most amazing place on Earth! We went rafting on the river. The red and brown canyon walls around us are taller than my house. The river took us over fast rapids. The water was very cold. It felt great in the hot sun.

EXPLORE AMAZING UTAH!

Today, we went hiking in the mountains near Four Corners. It was hot in the valley below. We walked for three hours to get to the top. It's so high up there! You can see for miles! It was much cooler, too. We even had to wear our jackets.

6

3

Arches National Monument,
Utah

Wow! This place is great. There
are thousands of big red rocks here.
Some look like skyscrapers and
bridges, too. You need to see them
sometime. I didn't want to leave.

Mesa Verde, Colorado

Today, we got to explore some cliff dwellings.
The Anasazi people built them hundreds of years
ago. There are many rooms in the cliffs. In fact,
the rooms form a village. There are ladders that
go into some of the rooms. Some rooms have
round towers.

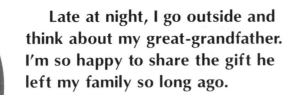

Late at night, I go outside and think about my great-grandfather. I'm so happy to share the gift he left my family so long ago.

Words with Prefixes and Suffixes

carefully	finally	refill	thankful
countless	fuzzy	reuse	tightly
cupfuls	gently	silently	unlike
endless	harmful	softly	unpack
family	helpful	sticky	unripe

High Frequency Words

as	beautiful	friends	outdoors
any	each	healthy	special
away	few	indoors	trees
back	form	near	warm

My family has a beautiful peach orchard. My great-grandfather planted the trees as a special gift to his family. Every summer, we all gather to pick the plump fruit from the trees. We are very thankful for the trees.

We boil the filled jars. This kills any harmful bacteria in the fruit. After the jars cool, we label each one.

Our canned fruit is unlike anything you buy in a store. Sometimes when we give a jar away, the people bring back the empty jar and ask for a refill!

Dad gently washes each peach. I peel the skin and remove the pits. Mom carefully packs the fruit into the jars and covers it with cupfuls of warm, sticky syrup. Then we screw on each lid tightly.

We wait all year for the peaches to grow. In the late winter, small pink buds appear on the trees. The flowers blossom. Then the petals fall off and float silently to the ground. In the spring, the fuzzy peaches start to form. We set up a big picnic table near the branches full of hard, unripe fruit. We all eat together under the shade of the trees.

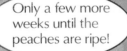

Only a few more weeks until the peaches are ripe!

We sit and listen. The leaves flutter softly in the wind. It is like Great-grandfather's voice whispering that we will soon enjoy his gift.

When summer is finally here, there is endless work outdoors. All of the family and countless friends arrive. Everyone is so helpful. We carry crates and pick the healthy fruit.

We have a lot of fresh peaches, so we put some in jars to enjoy in the winter.

When it's time to can the fruit, there is endless work indoors. We unpack boxes of glass jars that we reuse from year to year. We still have a few jars from when Great-grandmother canned peaches years ago!

4   **5**

Fold

The Geminids will come again next year, too. Look for them. If the sky is clear, you will be amazed, too!

Multisyllabic Words			
another	excited	Latin	suddenly
beneath	fantastic	looking	surprise
celebrate	Geminids	planet	surrounds
crashes	going	really	very
darkest	happen	season	whizzing
eleven	hardly	shooting	winter
enjoy	hundreds	shower	

High Frequency Words			
as	cold	if	right
because	earth	into	show
called	friends	know	watch
close	from	often	

Multisyllabic Words

Meteor Shower

It's the middle of the night on December 13. It is winter, the darkest season of the year. My friends wonder what I am going to show them. They grumble as we trudge up the steep hill.

It's too cold!

It's so dark!

What are we looking for?

What a fantastic way to celebrate the darkest season of the year! My friends and I will always remember this night.

Suddenly hundreds of meteors begin to shoot across the sky. It's like a fireworks display! My friends do not grumble anymore. They are really glad they came. We huddle beneath blankets and watch the amazing show.

I smile and lead them up the hill. I did not tell them what is going to happen. I want them to be surprised. I know they will enjoy the show. I check my watch. It's eleven p.m. The night sky will soon be filled with hundreds of shooting stars, or meteors, whizzing past the earth. I can hardly wait.

Meteors are bits of space dirt. They hurtle through space at great speeds. Some pass very close to Earth. They burn up in the layer of gas that surrounds the planet. Meteors look like bright balls of fire as they burn. Most burn out and then fall to the earth as dust.

Sometimes a meteor does not burn up and crashes into Earth with a great bang! That does not happen very often.

The meteor shower begins right on time. My friends are excited to see the first shooting star. I do not tell them that there will be more—many more.

These meteors are called Geminids because they appear to come from a group of stars called Gemini. I look in the sky for that group of stars. I tell my friends that Gemini means "The Twins" in Latin. I point to The Twins in the night sky.

Photographs

F2 Row 1: (l, lml) Getty Images, (ml) Digital Stock, (rmr, mr) Getty Images, (r) Artville. Row 2: (l) Ryan McVay/Getty Images, (m) Digital Stock, (r) Metaphotos. Row 3: (l) LWA/Getty Images, (m) Harald Sund/Getty Images, (r) Getty Images. Row 4: (l) Steve Cole/Getty Images, (m) Paul Beard/Getty Images, (r) Getty Images. **F3** Row 1: (l, m) Getty Images, (r) Paul Beard/Getty Images. Row 2: (l) Getty Images, (m) EyeWire, (r) Digital Stock. Row 3: (l) Getty Images, (m) Metaphotos, (r) Getty Images. Row 4: (l, m) Digital Stock, (r) Getty Images. Row 5: (l) Artville, (m) Steve Cole/Getty Images, (r) Getty Images. **F4** (tl, tr) Liz Garza Williams, (bl) Digital Stock, (br) Liz Garza Williams. **F5** Row 1: (l, r) Artville: Row 2: (l) Artville, (r) Liz Garza Williams. Row 3: (l, r) Artville. **F6** (t, m) Liz Garza Williams, (b) Artville. **F7** (t, m) Artville, (b) Liz Garza Williams. **F8** Row 1: (l) Artville. Row 2: (l) Getty Images, (r) Liz Garza Williams. Row 3: (l) Artville, (r) Liz Garza Williams. Row 4: (l) Liz Garza Williams, (r) Artville. Row 5: (l, r) Liz Garza Williams. **F9** Row 1: (l) Getty Images, (r) Liz Garza Williams. Row 2: (l) Liz Garza Williams. Row 3: (l) Artville, (r) Liz Garza Williams. Row 4: (l, r) Liz Garza Williams. **F10** Row 1: (l) Image Club, (ml) Janis Christie/Getty Images, (m) Artville, (mr) Liz Garza Williams, (r) John Paul Endress. Row 2: (l) Getty Images, (m) John Paul Endress, (r) Stockbyte. Row 3: (l) John Paul Endress, (m) Artville, (r) Stockbyte. Row 4: (l) Digital Stock, (m) Getty Images, (r) Liz Garza Williams. Row 5: (l) Artville, (m) John Paul Endress, (r) Liz Garza Williams. **F11** Row 1: (l) Artville, (m) D. Falconer/PhotoLink/Getty Images, (r) Getty Images. Row 2: (l) Getty Images, (m) Stockbyte/Getty Images, (r) Liz Garza Williams. Row 3: (l) John Paul Endress, (m) Stockbyte, (r) Liz Garza Williams. Row 4: (l) Liz Garza Williams, (m) Stockbyte, (r) Getty Images. **F15** (t-b) Stockbyte, John Paul Endress, New Century Graphics, Stockbyte/Getty Images. **F16** Row 1: (l) Liz Garza Williams, (r) D. Falconer/PhotoLink/Getty Images. Row 2: (l, r) Liz Garza Williams. Row 3: (l) Stockbyte, (r) John Paul Endress. Row 4: (l, ml) Getty Images, (mr) John Paul Endress, (r) D. Falconer/PhotoLink/Getty Images. Row 5: (l) Artville, (ml, mr, r) Liz Garza Williams, (br) Artville. **F17** Row 1: (l) Artville, (r) Stockbyte. Row 2: (l) Getty Images, (r) John Paul Endress. Row 3: (l) Liz Garza Williams, (r) D. Falconer/PhotoLink/Getty Images. Row 4: (l) Paul Beard/Getty Images, (ml) D. Falconer/PhotoLink/Getty Images, (mr, r) Liz Garza Williams, (r) Getty Images. Row 5: (l) Digital Stock, (ml) Stockbyte, (mr) Getty Images, (r) Liz Garza Williams. Row 6: (l, ml) Liz Garza Williams, (mr) Stockbyte/Getty Images, (r) Liz Garza Williams. **F18** Row 1: (l) Getty Images, (ml) Liz Garza Williams, (m) Getty Images, (mr) Artville, (r) Liz Garza Williams. Row 2: (l) SuperStock, Inc/SuperStock, (ml) John Paul Endress, (mr) Ryan McVay/Getty Images, (r) Image Club. Row 3: (l, ml) Artville, (mr) C Squared Studios/Getty Images, (r) John Paul Endress. Row 4: (l) John Paul Endress, (ml) Stockbyte, (mr) John Paul Endress, (r) Jack Fields/Corbis. Row 5: (l) Artville, (ml) Stockbyte, (mr) EyeWire, (r) Artville. **F19** Row 1: (l) John Paul Endress, (m) Artville, (r) Liz Garza Williams. Row 2: (l) Getty Images, (m) Digital Stock, (r) Stockbyte. Row 3: (l) Laura Dwight/Corbis, (m) Liz Garza Williams, (r) D. Falconer/PhotoLink/Getty Images. Row 4: (l, m) Getty Images, (r) John Paul Endress. **F20**

Liz Garza Williams. **F23** (t-b) Artville, Getty Images, Bill Aron/PhotoEdit, D. Falconer/PhotoLink/Getty Images, Liz Garza Williams. **F24** Row 1: (l) Liz Garza Williams, (m) Stockbyte, (r) Laura Dwight/Corbis. Row 2: (l) Getty Images, (m, r) John Paul Endress. Row 3: (l) Getty Images, (m) D. Falconer/PhotoLink/Getty Images, (r) Getty Images. Row 4: (l) Artville, (m) Thom Lang/Corbis. Row 5: (l, m) Getty Images, (r) Liz Garza Williams. **F25** Row 1: (l) Bill Aron/PhotoEdit, (m) John Paul Endress, (r) Liz Garza Williams. Row 2: (m) Stockbyte, (r) C Squared Studios/Getty Images. Row 3: (l) Laura Dwight/Corbis, (m, r) Artville. Row 4: (l) Laura Dwight/Corbis, (ml) Getty Images, (mr, r) Liz Garza Williams. Row 5: (l) D. Falconer/PhotoLink/Getty Images, (ml) Ryan McVay/Getty Images. Row 6: (l, ml) Getty Images, (mr) C Squared Studios/Getty Images, (r) Stockbyte/Getty Images. **F26** (l, m) Liz Garza Williams. (mr) Getty Images, (r) Digital Studios. **F27** Row 1: (l) Laura Dwight/Corbis, (m) John Paul Endress, (r) Liz Garza Williams. Row 2: (l) Liz Garza Williams, (m) John Paul Endress, (r) Getty Images. Row 3: (l) C Squared Studios/Getty Images, (m) Artville, (r) Charles Krebs/Getty Images. Row 4: (l) Digital Studios, (m) Duomo/Corbis, (r) Liz Garza Williams. **F31** (t) Duomo/Corbis, (m) C Squared Studios/Getty Images, (b) David Young-Wolff/PhotoEdit. **F32** Row 1: (l) C Squared Studios/Getty Images, (ml, mr) Liz Garza Williams, (r) David Young-Wolff/PhotoEdit. Row 2: (l, m) Artville, (r) C Squared Studios/Getty Images. Row 3: (l) John Paul Endress, (m, r) Getty Images. Row 4: (l, ml) Liz Garza Williams, (mr) Artville, (r) David Young-Wolff/PhotoEdit. Row 5: (m, r) Liz Garza Williams. Row 6: (l) D. Falconer/PhotoLink/Getty Images, (m) Ryan McVay/Getty Images, (r) Laura Dwight/Corbis. **F33** Row 1: (l, ml) Liz Garza Williams (mr) Getty Images, (r) John Paul Endress. Row 2: (l) Getty Images, (m) Bill Aron/PhotoEdit, (r) D. Falconer/PhotoLink/Getty Images. Row 3: (l) Getty Images, (m) Laura Dwight/Corbis, (r) Liz Garza Williams. Row 4: (l) Getty Images, (m) C Squared Studios/Getty Images, (r) Duomo/Corbis. Row 5: (l) Charles Krebs/Getty Images, (m) John Paul Endress, (r) Liz Garza Williams. Row 6: (l) David Young-Wolff/PhotoEdit, (m) Digital Stock, (r) Artville. **F34** (l-ml) John Paul Endress, (m) Image Library, (mr) Artville, (r) John Paul Endress. **F35** Row 1: (l) Liz Garza Williams, (m) Getty Images. Row 2: (l) Roger Ressmeyer/Corbis, (m) New Century Graphics, (r) John Paul Endress. Row 3: (l) Siede Preis/Getty Images, (m) Liz Garza Williams. Row 4: (l) John Paul Endress, (m) Liz Garza Williams, (r) Jack Fields/Corbis. **F39** (t-b) Roger Ressmeyer/Corbis, Liz Garza Williams, Jack Fields/Corbis, Getty Images, Liz Garza Williams, Paul Beard/Getty Images. **F40** Row 1: (l, m) Getty Images, (r) John Paul Endress, Row 2: (l) Ryan McVay/Getty Images, (m) Liz Garza Williams, (r) Siede Preis/Getty Images. Row 3: (l) Bill Aron/PhotoEdit, (r) Jack Fields/Corbis. Row 4: (l) Liz Garza Williams, (m) Roger Ressmeyer/Corbis, (r) John Paul Endress. Row 5: (l) Liz Garza Williams, (m) Getty Images, (r) D. Falconer/PhotoLink/Getty Images. **F41** Row 1: (m) Bill Aron/PhotoEdit, (r) Stockbyte. Row 2: (l-r) Getty Images. Row 3: (l) Getty Images, (m) C Squared Studios/Getty Images, (r) Getty Images. Row 4: (l) New Century Studios, (ml) Getty Images, (mr) Roger Ressmeyer/Corbis, (r) Artville. Row 5: (l, m) Liz Garza Williams, (r) Siede Preis/Getty Images. Row 6: (l) Liz Garza Williams, (ml) Paul

Beard/Getty Images, (mr) John Paul Endress, (r) Stockbyte. **3** Row 1: (l) Liz Garza Williams, (ml) Bill Aron/PhotoEdit, (mr) Laura Dwight/Corbis, (r) Getty Images. Row 2: (l) Liz Garza Williams, (ml, mr) Getty Images, (r) Stockbyte. Row 3: (m) Getty Images, (r) Liz Garza Williams. **4** Row 1: (l) Getty Images, (ml) Burke/Triolo Products/Brand X/Corbis, (mr, r) Getty Images. Row 2: (l) Bill Aron/PhotoEdit, (ml, mr, r) Getty Images. Row 3: (m, r) Getty Images. **5** Row 1: (l) Digital Stock, (ml) Getty Images, (m) John Paul Endress, (mr) Digital Stock. (r) Joel Satore/National Geographic Image Collection. Row 2: (l) William Salaza/Corbis, (ml) Artville, (m, mr) Getty Images, (r) Michael Jan/Getty Images. Row 3: (l) C Squared Studios/Getty Images, (ml) Getty Images, (m) Jack Fields/Corbis, (mr) Digital Stock, (r) Ryan McVay/Getty Images. Row 4: (l) Liz Garza Williams, (m) Artville, (r) Getty Image. **6** Row 1: (l) Artville, (ml) Getty Images, (m) Michael Yamashita/Corbis, (mr, r) Liz Garza Williams. Row 2: (l) Michael Jang/Getty Images. (ml) Bill Aron/PhotoEdit, (m) Getty Images, (mr) Bob Rowan/Corbis, (r) Getty Images. Row 3: (l) Digital Stock, (ml) James Balog/Getty Images, (m) Getty Images, (mr) Artville, (r) Duomo/Corbis. Row 4: (l, ml) Getty Images, (mr) C Squared Studios/Getty Images, (r) Getty Images. Row 5: (l) C Squared Studios/Getty Images, (ml) Burke/Triolo Productions/Brand X/Corbis, (mr) Michael Yamashita/Corbis, (r) Liz Garza Williams. **9** Row 1: (l) D. Falconer/PhotoLink/Getty Images, (ml, mr) Getty Images, (r) Liz Garza Williams. Row 2: (l) Digital Stock, (mr) Getty Images, (r) Liz Garza Williams. Row 3: (m, r) Liz Garza Williams. **10** (l) John Paul Endress, (ml) Liz Garza Williams, (mr) D. Falconer/PhotoLink/Getty Images, (r) Liz Garza Williams. Row 2: (l, ml) Getty Images, (mr) New Century Graphics, (r) Getty Images. Row 3: (m) Getty Images, (r) New Century Graphics. **11** Row 1: (l) John Paul Endress, (ml, m) Getty Images, (mr) Digital Stock, (r) John Paul Endress. Row 2: (l) John Paul Endress, (ml, m) Getty Images, (mr) John Paul Endress, (r) Getty Images. Row 3: (l) D. Falconer/PhotoLink/Getty Images, (ml) James Marshall/Corbis, (m) Getty Images, (mr) Javier Pierini/Getty Images, (r) New Century Graphics. Row 4: (l, ml) Liz Garza Williams, (mr) Alfred Gescheidt/Getty Images, (r) Artville. Row 6: (l) Getty Images, (m) Artville, (r) Getty Images. **12** Row 1: (l) John Paul Endress, (r) Liz Garza Williams. Row 2: (l) Liz Garza Williams. Row 3: (l, r) Liz Garza Williams. Row 4: (l) Getty Images, (ml) Liz Garza Williams, (mr) Getty Images, (r) D. Falconer/PhotoLink/Getty Images. Row 5: (l) Stockbyte/Getty Images, (ml) Liz Garza Williams, (mr) John Paul Endress, (r) Liz Garza Williams. Row 6: (l) Getty Images, (ml) John Paul Endress, (mr) Digital Stock, (r) Paul Beard/Getty Images. **15** Row 1: (l) Digital Studios, (m) John Paul Endress, (r) Steve Cole/Getty Images, Row 2: (l) Liz Garza Williams, (m) Getty Images, (r) Stockbyte/Getty Images. Row 3: (l) Charles Krebs/Getty Images, (m) Getty Images, (r) Liz Garza Williams. **16** Row 1: (l) Myrleen Ferguson Cate/PhotoEdit, (ml) David Young-Wolff/PhotoEdit. (mr, r) Artville. Row 2: (l) John Paul Endress, (ml) Louis Grandadam/Getty Images, (mr) LWA-Dann Tardif/Corbis, (r) David Hanover/Getty Images. Row 3: (l, ml) Liz Garza Williams, (mr) John Paul Endress, (r) Michael Newman/PhotoEdit. Row 4: (l) David Frazier/Corbis, (m) Getty Images. **17** Row 1: (l) Getty Images, (ml, mr, r) John Paul Endress. Row 2: (l) Joel Sartore/

National Geographic Image Collection, (ml) Eising Food Photography/StockFood, (mr) Peter Correz/Getty Images, (r) EyeWire. Row 3: (l) Robert Bremnel/PhotoEdit, (ml) Bob Elsdale/Getty Images, (mr) Joel Sartore/National Geographic Image Collection, (r) EyeWire. Row 4: (l) Artville, (m) John Paul Endress. **18** Row 1: (l) Liz Garza Williams, (m) Getty Images, (r) Siede Preis/Getty Images. Row 2: (l) Steve Mason/Getty Images, (m) Getty Images, (r) Digital Stock. **21** Row 1: (l) Getty Images, (ml) C Squared Studios/Getty Images, (mr) Getty Images, (r) Artville. Row 2: (l) Steve Mason/Getty Images, (ml) Getty Images, (mr) Michael Jang/Getty Images, (r) Jules Frazier/Getty Images. **22** Row 1: (l) John Paul Endress, (m) Stockbyte, (r) Getty Images. Row 2: (l) Getty Images, (m) Digital Stock, (r) Paul Beard/Getty Images. **23** Row 1: (l) Digital Stock, (ml) Leonard de Selva/Corbis, (mr) Artville, (r) Getty Images. Row 2: (l) Getty Images, (ml) Digital Stock, (mr) Siede Preis/Getty Images, (r) Phillippa Lewis/Edivice/Corbis. **26** Row 1: (l) Jon Smyth/SuperStock, (m) Artville, (r) Barbara Penoyar/Getty Images. Row 2: (l) Carl & Ann Purcell/Corbis, (m) John Paul Endress, (r) Digital Stock. Row 3: (m) Carl & Ann Purcell/Corbis, (r) John Paul Endress. **27** (l) Getty Images, (ml, mr) Liz Garza Williams, (r) Stockbyte/Getty Images. **28** (tl) Getty Images, (tc) John Paul Endress, (tr) John Foster/Photo Researchers, Inc., (ml) John Paul Endress, (mc) Stockbyte, (mr) Image Club, (bc) John Paul Endress, (br) Stockbyte. **29** Row 1: (l, ml) Artville, (mr) Digital Studios, (r) Getty Images. Row 2: (l) Leonard de Selva/Corbis, (ml) Artville, (mr) New Century Graphics, (r) Michael Newman/PhotoEdit. **32** Row 1: (l) Metaphotos, (ml) Robert Daly/Getty Images, (mr) C Squared Studios/Getty Images, (r) Artville. Row 2: (l) Spike Mafford/Getty Images, (ml) John Paul Endress, (mr) Getty Images, (r) Image Library. Row 3: (m) Artville, (r) Spike Mafford/Getty Images. **33** Row 1: (l) Stephen Simpson/Getty Images, (ml) Artville, (mr, r) Getty Images. Row 2: (l) Getty Images, (ml) Artville, (mr) Roderick Chen/Super/Stock, (r) John Paul Endress. Row 3: (m) Stephen Simpson/Getty Images, (r) Getty Images. Row 4: (m) Artville, (r) Getty Images. **34** Row 1: (l) Ryan McVay/Getty Images, (ml) John Paul Endress, (mr) Roderick Chen/SuperStock, (r) Michale Dunn/Corbis. Row 2: (l) Getty Images, (ml) Liz Garza Williams, (mr) Nancy R. Cohen/Getty Images, (r) Metaphotos. Row 3: (m) Getty Images, (r) Nancy R. Cohen/Getty Images. Row 4: (m) Roderick Chen/SuperStock, (r) John Paul Endress. **35** Row 1: (l) Liz Garza Williams, (ml, mr) Getty Images, (r) James Forte/Getty Images. Row 2: (tl, l) Getty Images, (ml) Artville, (mr) Liz Garza Williams, (r) Getty Images. **38** Row 1: (l, m) Getty Images, (r) Liz Garza Williams, Row 2: (l) Liz Garza Williams, (m) Artville, (r) Bruce Hands/Getty Images. Row 3: (m) Getty Images, (r) Liz Garza Williams. **39** Row 1: (l) Getty Images, (ml) Artville, (m) Onne van der Wal/Corbis, (mr) Jerry Tobias/Corbis, (r) Liz Garza Williams. Row 2: (l) Bruce Hands/Getty Images, (ml, m) Getty Images, (mr) Purestock/SuperStock, (r) Felicia Martinez/PhotoEdit. Row 3: (l) Arthur C. Smith III/Grant Heilman Photography, (ml) Joe Munroe/Photo Researchers, Inc. (m) Don Mason/Brand X/Jupiter Images, (mr) Digital Stock, (r) Corel. Row 4: (m) SuperStock, (r) Ariel Skelley/Corbis. **40** Row 1: (l) Getty Images, (ml) Roderick Chen/SuperStock, (mr) David Young-Wolff/PhotoEdit, (r) Corel. Row 2: (l) Getty Images, (ml) Okapia Frankfurt/Photo Researchers Inc., (mr) Digital Stock, (r) Nancy R.

Cohen/Getty Images. Row 3: (m) Roderick Chen/SuperStock, (r) Getty Images. **41** Row 1: (l) John Paul Endress, (ml) Don Mason/Brand X/Jupiter Images, (mr) Ariel Skelley/Corbis, (r) Bruce Hands/Getty Images. Row 2: (l) Digital Stock, (ml) Siede Preis/Getty Images, (mr) Warren Bolster/Getty Images, (r) Pat O'Hara/Corbis. **48** (tl) Ariel Skelley/Corbis, (ml, bl) Getty Images. **51** Row 1: (l, m) Artville, (r) Liz Garza Williams. Row 2: (l) Digital Vision, (m) Duomo/Corbis. Row 3: (m) Artville, (r) Liz Garza Williams. **52** Row 1: (l) Artville, (m) John Paul Endress, (r) Artville. Row 2: (l) J. A. Kraulis/Masterfile, (m) John Foster/Photo Researchers, Inc. (r) John Paul Endress. Row 3: (m) J. A. Kraulis/Masterfile, (r) John Paul Endress. **55** Row 1: (l) VisionsofAmerica/Joe Sohm/Getty Images, (lm) Jules Frazier/Getty Images, (rm) Artville, (r) Getty Images. Row 2: (l) Artville, (ml) Stockbyte, (mr) Siede Preis/Getty Images, (r) Chat Roberts/Corbis/Jupiter Images, (bc) Artville, (br) Siede Preis/Getty Images. **56** Row 1: (l) John Paul Endress, (ml) Getty Images, (mr) Jess Alford/Getty Images, (r) Artville. Row 2: (l) Barbara Penoyer/Getty Images, (ml) Siede Preis/Getty Images, (mr) Getty Images, (r) Lee Snider/Corbis. Row 3: (m) Siede Preis/Getty Images, (r) Getty Images. Row 4: (m) Artville, (r) Barbara Penoyar/Getty Images. **57** Row 1: (l) Getty Images, (ml) Plush Studios/Getty Images, (mr) Chat Roberts/Corbis/Jupiter Images, (r) Getty Images. Row 2: (l) Liz Garza Williams, (ml) Stockbyte, (mr) Getty Images, (r) Jess Alford/Getty Images. Row 3: (mr) Plush Studios/Getty Images, (r) Jess Alford/Getty Images. Row 4: (mr) Chat Roberts/Corbis/Jupiter Images, (r) Liz Garza Williams. **58** Row 1: (l) Ryan McVay/Getty Images, (ml) Paul Dance/Getty Images, (mr) Francisco Erize/Bruck Coleman Inc., (r) Ryan McVay/Getty Images. Row 2: (l, ml) Getty Images, (mr) Artville, (r) Jules Frazier/Getty Images. Row 3: (m) Ryan McVay/Getty Images, (r) Paul Dance/Getty Images. Row 4: (m) Ryan McVay/Getty Images, (r) Artville. **61** Row 1: (l) Digital Vision/Getty Images, (ml) 1999-2000 Getty Images, Inc., (mr, r) John Paul Endress. Row 2: (l) Freeman Patterson/Masterfile, (ml) David Sailors, (mr) Getty Images, (r) Brian Hagiwara/PhotoPix/Jupiter Images. **64** Row 1: (l) Peter Gridley/Getty Images, (m) VisionsofAmerica/Joe Sohm/Getty Images, (r) Corbis. Row 2: (l) Paul Thomas/Getty Images, (m, r) John Paul Endress. Row 3: (m) Corbis, (r) VisionsofAmerica/Joe Sohm/Getty Images. **68** Row 1: (l) Barbara Penoyar/Getty Images, (m) Artville, (r) John Smyth/SuperStock. Row 2: (l) John Paul Endress, (m) Carl & Ann Purcell/Corbis, (r) Digital Stock. Row 3: (m) Carl & Ann Purcell/Corbis, (r) John Paul Endress. **69** Row 1: (l) Barbara Penoyar/Getty Images, (ml) C Squared Studios/Getty Images, (m) Getty Images, (mr) John Smyth/SuperStock, (r) Carl & Ann Purcell/Corbis. Row 2: (l) Ron Chapple/Thinkstock/Jupiter Images, (ml) John Paul Endress, (m) Getty Images, (mr) Artville, (r) Peter Byron/PhotoEdit. Row 3: (l) Getty Images, (ml) Ken Giese/SuperStock, (m) Digital Stock, (mr) Liz Garza Williams, (r) Tony Freeman/PhotoEdit. **70** Row 1: (l) Getty Images, (m,r) John Paul Endress. Row 2: (l) John Paul Endress, (m) Stockbyte, (r) John Foster/Photo Researchers. Row 3: (m) John Paul Endress, (r) Stockbyte. **71** Row 1: (l, ml) Getty Images, (m) Stockbyte, (mr) Artville, (r) Corbis/Jupiter Images. Row 2: (l) John Paul Endress, (ml) Rita Maas/Getty Images, (m) Mike McQueen/Getty Images, (mr) John Paul Endress, (r) David Young-Wolff/PhotoEdit. Row 3: (l)

C Squared Studios/Getty Images, (ml) John Foster/Photo Researchers, (m) Ryan McVay/Getty Images, (mr) Jules Frazier/Getty Images, (r) John Paul Endress. **74** Row 1: (l) Digital Stock, (m) John Paul Endress, (r) Artville. Row 2: (l, m) Getty Images, (r) Ryan McVay/Getty Images. Row 3: (m) Digital Stock, (r) Getty Images. **75** Row 1: (l) Ryan McVay/Getty Images, (ml) Getty Images, (mr) Lawrence Lawry/Getty Images, (r) Digital Stock. Row 2: (l) Getty Images, (ml) Jonathan Nourok/PhotoEdit, (mr) John Paul Endress, (r) Liz Garza Williams. Row 3: (l) Artville, (ml) Getty Images, (mr) John Paul Endress, (r) GeoStock/Getty Images. Row 4: (l) Zoran Milich/Masterfile, (ml) Getty Images, (mr) Liz Garza Williams, (r) Robert Daly/Getty Images. **76** (tl) Getty Images, (tc) Getty Images, (ml) Liz Garza Williams, (mc) Getty Images, (mr) Liz Garza Williams. **77** Row 1: (l, ml) Artville, (mr, r) Getty Images. Row 2: (l, ml, mr) Getty Images, (r) Donald Specker/Animals Animals-Earth Scenes. Row 3: (mr, r) Artville. **78** (mr) David Muench/Corbis. **80** Row 1: (l) C Squared Studios/Getty Images, (ml) Howard Folsom/PictureQuest/Jupiter Images, (mr) Phil Borden/PhotoEdit, (r) Rita Maas/Getty Images. Row 2: (l) Getty Images, (ml) Camille Tokrud/Getty Images, (mr) Liz Garza Williams, (r) John Paul Endress. **81** Row 1: (l) Bettmann/Corbis, (ml) PhotoSphere Images/PictureQuest, (mr) Artville, (r) Robert Daly/Getty Images. Row 2: (l) Getty Images, (ml) D. Ducros/Photo Researchers, Inc., (mr) Digital Stock, (r) Digital Vision/PictureQuest. **84** (tl) Datacraft/Getty Images, (tc) John Paul Endress, (tr) Richard Hutchings/Corbis, (ml) Grant Heilman Photography, (mc) Blend Images/Jupiter Images, (mr) Barbara Peacock/Getty Images. **85** (tl) Tom Bean/Getty Images, (tc) Bettmann/Corbis, (tr) Authur S. Aubry/Getty Images, (ml) David Young-Wolff/PhotoEdit, (mc) Bonnie Kamin/Photo Edit, (mr) Tom Brakefeld/Getty Images. **86** (tl) John Paul Endress, (tc) Myrleen Ferguson Cate/PhotoEdit, (tr) Corbis, (ml) Image Club, (mc) Liz Garza Williams, (mr) Getty Images. **89** Row 1: (l) Artville, (ml) Getty Images, (mr) John Running, (r) Getty Images. Row 2: (l, ml, r) Getty Images. **90** Row 1: (l) Getty Images, (ml) Diego Azubel/epa/Corbis, (mr) Layne Kennedy/Corbis, (r) Steph Fowler/Brand X/Jupiter Images. Row 2: (l) David Young-Wolff/Getty Images, (ml) John Paul Endress, (mr) Tom Stewart/Corbis, (r) Bill Bachmann/PhotoEdit. **91** Row 1: (l) Getty Images, (ml) Diane Macdonald/Getty Images, (mr) Tom Stewart/Corbis, (r) Burke/Triolo Prouductions/Brand X/Jupiter Images. Row 2: (l) Getty Images, (ml) Corbis, (mr) Getty Images, (r) VCL/Spencer Rowell/Getty Images.

Illustrations

F8, F9 Liisa Chauncy Guida. **F26** Chi Chung. **9** Judith DuFour. **39** Alex von Dallwitz. **44-45** Maurie Manning. **49, 61** Judith DuFour Love. **131-154** Dick Smolinski. **155-158** Lee Woolry. **159-162** Dick Smolinski. **163-166** Den Schofield. **167-170** Frank Sofo. **171-174** Marcia J. Bateman Walker. **175-178** Lee Woolry. **179-182** Ken Stetz. **183-186** Lee Woolry. **187-190** Frank Sofo. **191-194** Stephen Wells. **195-198** Lee Woolry. **199-202** Den Schofield.